# NEW HOMES
## and
# POOR PEOPLE

## A Study of Chains of Moves

**John B. Lansing**
**Charles Wade Clifton**
**James N. Morgan**

**SURVEY RESEARCH CENTER**

INSTITUTE FOR SOCIAL RESEARCH
THE UNIVERSITY OF MICHIGAN
ANN ARBOR, MICHIGAN

# Preface

The quality and quantity of housing available to the population are matters of continuing public concern. Provision of housing for the economically disadvantaged segments of the population is an especially important objective. Principal reliance for the provision of housing in the United States is placed on private enterprise guided by the processes of the market for housing. It is a matter of established policy that there is public intervention in the market, however, in ways ranging from mortgage insurance to tax incentives to direct subsidy. Yet the workings of the housing market are too little understood for effective policy formulation. It is the objective of this study to contribute to knowledge of the working of the housing market.

The focus of this project is on the indirect consequences of new construction. When new housing units are built and occupied for the first time, the families which move into them usually free their former residences for occupancy by others. These others, in turn, may free other homes. The properties of the sequences of moves thus begun are the subject of this report.

The purpose of the study is to answer such questions as the following: What is the economic level of the people who move into new housing? If rich people move into new housing, do poor people benefit indirectly by moving into vacancies farther along in the sequences? Or, do the sequences stop before they reach low income people? If low income whites benefit, do low income Negroes also benefit by moving into the vacancies? Are sequences which start with expensive housing longer than those which start with moderate priced housing?

A sample of new dwelling units in metropolitan areas was the starting point of the research. The data collection has consisted in interviewing the first people to live in each new housing unit in this sample and also the people who now live in the units left vacant by those who moved into the new units, and so on. As will be described in detail, each sequence of moves has been followed, if possible, to its logical conclusion, that is, until a dwelling is removed from the housing supply, or is occupied by people who left no vacancy for someone else to fill.

The selection of new dwelling units for inclusion in this project was made on the basis of a list of building permit numbers showing permit office and date issued for each of the areas in the sample. This list was made available to us by the U.S. Bureau of the Census. We wish to acknowledge gratefully the assistance of the staff of the Bureau in the selection of the sample.

The sample was designed to take advantage of this assistance, and is not a strict probability sample of primary sampling units. Roughly speaking, the universe represented is all standard metropolitan statistical areas in the U.S. with a population of 200,000 or more in the central city. The sample of new construction includes new dwellings in 17 geographical areas. Interviews were taken in other parts of the country where necessary in order to follow chains of moves involving people who migrated.

Interviews were successfully completed at 1133 newly occupied homes. Occasionally two vacancies arise when people who have been maintaining separate homes combine forces and occupy a third home. It has been convenient in some tabulations to treat these situations as if there were two separate sequences of moves. On this basis there were 1144 sequences. Including interviews at subsequent steps in the sequences of moves, a total of 2651 interviews were taken between July 1 and December 31, 1966. A special effort was made the following summer to learn as much as possible about sequences for which the information obtained in the fall of 1966 was incomplete. This effort resulted in an additional 390 interviews in the same sequences in July and August 1967. The revised total number of interviews in the project is 3039, allowing for the exclusion from the final count of 2 interviews taken in 1966 which the subsequent investigation showed should not have been taken. This report is based on these 3039 interviews.

These interviews have not carried to their logical conclusion all of the 1144 sequences. Interviews were completed with 88.5 percent of all eligible respondents in the new homes. Estimates will be presented of the characteristics of the sequences of moves as they would appear if there had been no interviewing failures. These estimates imply that 85.7 percent of all families in the sequences begun by the 1133 homes were interviewed.

This report stresses the question of whether the housing market operates in such a way that new construction indirectly benefits the poor in general and Negroes in particular. It also exploits the material collected in this study to contribute to understanding of the demand for new housing.

A second report is planned and is being prepared by one of the authors, Charles Wade Clifton. This report will present a theoretical model of the housing market as a whole developed in response to the problems posed by the present approach. It will also consider in some detail the income elasticity of the demand for housing and the problem, here treated rather arbitrarily, of how to equate house value and monthly rent.

This project was financed by a grant from the Ford Foundation. We wish to acknowledge the contributions to the formulation of the project made by Louis Winnick of the staff of the Foundation. He called to our attention the pioneering study of chains of moves by Frank S. Kristof.[1]

This project was planned jointly by the three authors. Supervision of the data collection and coding, and the development and preparation of tables were primarily the responsibility of Charles Wade Clifton. The text of this report has been written primarily by John B. Lansing.

We also wish to acknowledge the contributions of other members of the staff of the Survey Research Center. The Center is a division of the Institute for Social Research of The University of Michigan. The Director of the Institute is Rensis Likert; of the Survey Research Center, Angus Campbell; of the Economic Behavior Program, George Katona. The responsibility for the selection of the sample was carried by the Sampling Section of the Survey Research Center under the direction of Irene Hess. Staff of the Sampling Section specially assigned to this study included Thomas Tharakan. Appendix A in particular is based on the work of the Sampling Section. Interviewing was carried out by the Field Staff of the Survey Research Center under the direction of John Scott. Jeanette Rusk and Jeanne Keresztesi of the Field Office were especially active on the study. The coding of the project was under the supervision of Joan Scheffler. The Data Processing Facility of the Institute is under the direction of John Sonquist. Gary Hendricks and Janet Keller assisted in the preparation of the manuscript. We are especially indebted to Shorey Peterson for a critical reading of drafts of this report. The manuscript was typed by Anita Grob.

---

[1]Frank S. Kristof, "Housing Policy Goals and the Turnover of Housing," Journal of the American Institute of Planners, August 1965, pp. 232-245.

# Contents

# 1
# Introduction:
# The Moves Induced By
# New Construction

THE underlying purpose of this investigation is to contribute to intelligent formulation of public policy toward housing. The central concern in the development and conduct of the research has been the broad question: how do measures which have their initial impact on new construction indirectly influence the supply of housing available to people who cannot afford to live in new houses? Although the study aims to illuminate aspects of the housing market in a manner useful for policy, no attempt will be made to relate the findings to particular policies, such as mortgage insurance, rent subsidy, zoning laws, open occupancy, and so on.

A brief, preliminary sketch of the workings of the housing market may serve to place this investigation in context. We begin with a simple model which assumes a static population, constant incomes and prices, and that new homes are initially quite expensive. Most new dwellings, like most new cars, go directly to high income people. Since buildings are durable most people will live in used housing. What type of housing people seek will depend on their incomes and their stage in the family life cycle. During its life a dwelling will be occupied by several families, and its aging, except for occasional renovation, will mean that they are successively less well served. Even under these assumptions dwellings that are built for the well-to-do, and thus are fairly large, are likely to be broken into apartments as they grow older.[1] New construction in a sense will balance

---

[1]The subdivision of old units is more likely if we relax the assumption of constant prices and take into account the secular rise in the price of lumber. Many of the older wooden houses in the United States were built for well-to-do families when lumber was cheap, and were scaled accordingly.

demolition, but the number of new units constructed will not exactly equal the number of units demolished owing to the subdivision of some units during their lifetime.

A way of viewing the utilization of old dwellings is to observe the sequences of moves occasioned by initial vacancies. Initial vacancies may result from new construction, with families vacating existing dwellings as they occupy new homes; or initial vacancies may come through the attrition of families from death, aging, or emigration. In either case filling an initial vacancy usually will leave a second vacancy, and a succession of related moves develops. In this process families satisfy their needs for more suitable housing, and an aging housing supply is reallocated. Housing initially superior may be said to "trickle-down" so that finally it is occupied by poor families at a cost they can manage. (In this report we define "families" to include unrelated individuals.)

To take account of population growth, rising incomes, and the construction of low-cost new homes, we must modify this description of the market. With more families and with greater desire to avoid crowding and to live separately, even in the case of widows and bachelors, new construction may need to exceed demolition by a substantial margin. New family units at each economic level will absorb some, perhaps most, of the vacancies that are created as a result of new construction for those at the top. The passing on of dwellings to new occupants will serve less adequately to accommodate families lower on the income scale. New construction will need to be designed for relatively lower income groups than under the former static assumptions. But the succession of moves occasioned by new construction may still be a major source of supply to the poor if the market works properly.

It is possible to envisage a situation, however, in which the successions of moves occasioned by new construction all come to an end before vacancies appear which are within the reach of poor families. There might be enough expansion of demand by people in the middle and upper income groups to fill all the vacancies. The people in the lower income groups would then benefit from new construction only in the wry sense that without it they would find more prosperous families bidding against them for the poor quarters they now occupy. Whether the facts fit this gloomy picture is a matter for empirical inquiry. A further important question is the extent to which benefits from new construction extend to Negroes, who may be disadvantaged both by low incomes and by racial discrimination in the housing market.

This project concentrates on the sequences of moves originated by new construction. There must also be explicit recognition of the second basic way in which successions of moves begin: by the normal attrition of the population through aging and death. Furthermore, in any complete accounting of the population of housing units there must be recognition of the fact that dwelling units are sometimes subdivided as they are passed along, and also occasionally combined into larger units during the lifetime of a structure.

There have been earlier studies of sequences of moves. The project which directly influenced this one was carried out by Frank S. Kristof in New York City as mentioned in the *Preface*[2]. This pioneering project was based on a sample of only 64 initially-occupied new units. No claims were made that the sample was representative of New York; and, even if it were, the unique character of that city, including its system of rent control, would make generalization hazardous. Kristof found that for every 10 newly constructed units in his sample 24 families were able to make adjustments in their housing circumstances.

There is also a theoretical literature on the housing market in which the "filtering process" and "trickle-down" are discussed.[3] Two approaches to the analysis of filtering have been distinguished. In one approach the focus is on the dwelling unit and on analysis of its history. Thus, a particular dwelling unit may be said to filter down over the years as it gets older and its market value or price falls. In the second approach the focus is on people, and how people of successively lower economic position obtain dwellings. Following the first approach, filtering may be defined in terms of a change in the selling price (or rent) of the dwelling unit, measured in constant dollars; or it may be defined in terms of changes in the rank order of the dwelling unit among all dwelling units when ranked by quality. Following the second, it may be defined in terms of the income level in absolute terms of the people who live in the dwelling, or their rank position among all income receiving units. Thus, a dwelling which at one time was occupied by a family in the top tenth of the income distribution may, after a long history, be the home of a family in the bottom tenth.

Approximately this distinction will be followed in the two chapters which follow this *Introduction*. Chapter II describes the succession of housing units involved in sequences of moves. It considers the rent or selling price of successive dwellings, the termination of sequences of moves, and the length of the sequences.

Chapter III is concerned with the characteristics of the *people* involved in the successive occupancies. It begins with the occupants of the new housing. Comparison is made of people's tenure before and after they move. Their stage in the family life cycle is obviously relevant to their needs for housing and to how crowded they may be. Their socio-economic status, as measured by their income and education, is carefully considered. Special emphasis is given to the

[2] Frank S. Kristof, "Housing Policy Goals and the Turnover of Housing," Journal of the American Institute of Planners, August 1965, pp. 232-245.

[3] See, for example, W. G. Grigsby, Housing Markets and Public Policy, Philadelphia, University of Pennsylvania Press, 1963. See especially Chapter 3. See also Ernest M. Fisher and Louis Winnick, "A Reformulation of the Filtering Concept," Journal of Social Issues, 1951, pp. 47-58.

housing of Negroes.

Chapter IV considers the sequences of moves arising from new construction in the context of national statistics on the entire housing market. Chapter V states the main conclusions reached in the study concerning the filtering process and the housing of the poor. Readers who wish to learn quickly the main facts about what was done in this project and what were the main findings may find their needs met by reading this introductory chapter plus Chapter V. Details concerning the method employed in the collection of data are presented in *Appendix A* and *Appendix B*. *Appendix C* describes the use of temporary quarters by people in a state of transition between homes. Only summary statistics and tables closely related to the text are presented in Chapters I-V; most of the supporting tables, which are listed in *Appendix D*, have been placed in *Appendix E*.

# 2
# The Housing Units Involved In
# The Sequences Of Moves

THE successive housing units involved in the sequences of moves which begin with occupancy of a new unit ought to be characterized by successively lower values, on the average, if filtering down is taking place. Whether the facts match this expectation requires examination of the data. It is also essential to an understanding of the indirect effects of new construction to know in some detail what brings sequences of moves to an end, and how many housing units are included in an average sequence. Differences in length of sequence may exist which are systematically related to the characteristics of the initial, new housing unit. Dwellings at different positions in the sequences may differ systematically in their location within a metropolitan area. These topics will be considered in this chapter, postponing until Chapter III consideration of the income level, race, and other characteristics of the occupants of the housing units.

## A. The Rent or Selling Price of Successive Dwellings

The investigation of the prices of successive dwelling units in chains of moves begun by new construction is complicated by the fact that a dwelling unit may change from owner-occupied to tenant-occupied. We shall consider the frequency of such transitions in Chapter III. To estimate change in "price" for a transition requires attention both to problems of capitalization and to the exact details of what is covered by rent, for which satisfactory data are lacking. We can obtain a reasonably good idea of the price of housing at successive positions, however, by considering the prices of owner-occupied and rental housing separately. Thus, we shall examine separately homes which were owner-occupied after the moves which we have been studying and those which were tenant-occupied.

We consider, first, owner-occupied homes. We are interested in differences in value from position to position. A starting point is the distribution of the new homes by value, which may be compared to the distribution for all owner-occupied homes in metropolitan areas. Nine out of ten of the new homes in this study have a reported value of $15,000 or above, leaving only 9 percent in the range $10,000-14,999, and practically none below $10,000. Of *all* owner-occupied homes in metropolitan areas, however, as shown in a complete survey, 20 percent are valued by the owner below $10,000, and 23 percent between $10,000 and $14,999, with only 57 percent valued over $15,000 (Appendix Table E-1). The mean house value for all owner-occupied homes is $17,900; the median, $16,000.[1] Clearly, there is a tendency for new homes to be priced above existing homes — as would be expected.

Furthermore there is indeed a tendency for the prices of homes to vary with the position of the dwellings in the sequence of moves as shown in Appendix Table E-2 and summarized in Graph 1. The mean falls from $25,900 at position one to $19,700 for position three and continues to decline slowly for positions four and beyond. It is influenced by the virtual absence of very high priced homes at these positions.

GRAPH 1

MEAN VALUE OF OWNER-OCCUPIED HOMES AT DIFFERENT POSITIONS
IN SEQUENCES OF MOVES

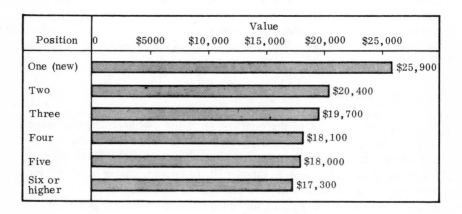

---

[1]These statistics were obtained from the 1966 Survey of Consumer Finances and based on 1038 interviews.

The distributions of monthly rent behave in a roughly similar manner. For new units, 81 percent of the renters are paying $100 or more, compared to only 19 percent of all renting nonfarm families and 21 percent of rent-paying families in metropolitan areas. New apartments typically are priced well above existing apartments (Appendix Table E-3). There is a strong tendency for monthly rents to decline from one position to the next (Appendix Table E-4). The mean rent for dwellings at different positions is shown in Graph 2. As

GRAPH 2

MEAN RENT OF RENTAL UNITS AT DIFFERENT POSITIONS
IN SEQUENCES OF MOVES

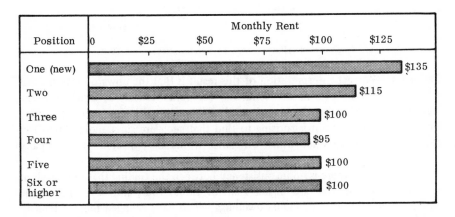

before, the mean falls from position to position but mean rent stabilizes at about the third position in the sequence.

We may compare these average rents with the distribution for all rent-paying families in all metropolitan areas. The mean rent for such families estimated from the 1966 Survey of Consumer Finances is $75; the median, $70.[2] Only 21 percent of all such families pay $100 or above (Appendix Tables E-3 and E-5), compared to 81 percent of those at position one.

These comparisons of value and rent by position number indicate what happens as sequences of moves develop. But they do not provide answers to questions about changes in price for each dwelling. Long term trends in value for individual housing units cannot be obtained from a cross-section survey such as is reported here, but it is possible to examine what happens to rental property between two occupancies. Increases in rent turn out to be more common than decreases. A comparison of rents has been prepared based on the intervals of

---

[2]Special tabulation from the 1966 Survey of Consumer Finances, based on 616 rent-paying families.

Appendix Table E-3, that is, intervals of $50. Of the new occupants 20 percent report being in a higher rent interval than was reported by the former tenants, compared to 11 percent who report lower rent, as the following tabulation shows:

| Comparison of Rent for the Same Dwelling | Percent |
|---|---|
| New renters two brackets higher (or more) | 3 |
| New renters one bracket higher | 17 |
| Same rent, within brackets | 69 |
| New renters one bracket lower | 9 |
| New renters two brackets lower (or less) | 2 |
| Total | 100 |
| Number of dwellings rented by two families | 1010 |

Perhaps the correct interpretation of this result is that the upward movement of prices more than offsets the tendency for rents to fall as units age. The movement of prices in general and building costs in particular has been upward in recent years. It is not surprising to find that such pressures more than offset the slow decline in value which otherwise would be expected to accompany aging.

Note that there is no inconsistency between the finding that rent levels at positions one and two are higher than at three, four, and beyond, and the finding that rents for individual dwellings which have changed tenants tend to move upward in absolute amount. Upward movement in the prices of older units still leaves their prices well below the prices of new units.

How are these higher prices paid? There must be an upward movement in movers' expenditure for housing in order both to cover the higher prices charged for the same housing when it changes hands and to allow for upgrading, that is, for the fact that housing units at the early positions in the sequence of moves are more expensive after the moves than those at the later positions. An estimate of the ratio of expenditures after the move to those before the move has been prepared on an approximate basis. For all families the median ratio is 127, meaning that the typical family pays about a quarter more after the move. For families moving into new housing units the ratio is 139. Another way of looking at the distribution of ratios for these families is to note that 44 percent of them are paying at least 50 percent more for housing after the move (see Appendix Table E-6).

These ratios are approximations. The problem is that of equivalence between rent and house value. If a family which was paying $100 rent buys a home for $10,000, what is its ratio of expenditures? In the construction of the set of equivalences used the rule was adopted that monthly rent is 1 percent of house value up to a value of $10,000. For higher valued homes a lower percentage was taken to be applicable. (The equivalences used are shown in the footnote to Appendix Table E-6.)

For families who did not change tenure status it is possible to compare directly the price paid for their present home to the price paid for their former home. When this relation is considered separately for owners and renters, omitting those who changed tenure status, the results are strongly in the direction of increased outlay after the move. Of owners, about 70 percent report a higher valued house after the move; of renters, half report rents which fall into a higher bracket, as is shown in Appendix Table E-7.

These results show that the finding that most people's outlay for housing increases when they move is not just a result of the rules adopted in this study about how to handle equivalences between rents and house values. The data do meet the test of logical consistency which requires that, given both higher prices for old housing and upgrading, families who move must increase their expenditures for housing.

## B. How the Sequences End

Logically, as already remarked, there are two reasons why the sequences of moves begun by the construction of new dwelling units come to an end. First, when the last occupants have moved out of the last dwelling unit in a sequence it may be removed from the stock of housing. It is then impossible for another family to move in. Second, the people who move into the dwelling at the last position in the sequence may leave no vacancy behind them even when the stock of housing does not change. Each of these possibilities requires further specification.

There are several ways in which a unit may be removed from the stock. The structure may be physically destroyed, either accidentally, by fire, storm, or other disaster, or deliberately. For example, a unit may be destroyed to clear a site for construction of a highway, park, or shopping center. Even though a structure continues to exist it may no longer be available as part of the stock of housing. It may be converted to non-residential purposes. It may continue as a residence but be used exclusively for seasonal occupancy, thereby disappearing from the stock of housing available for year-round occupancy. For example, a farmer in hill country may move to a city, selling his house to someone who wants a summer home. It is fairly common for large homes to be divided into apartments, which adds to the number of housing units, but it is also possible for this process to be reversed. One unit must be subtracted from the stock when one large dwelling is constructed from two smaller units during remodeling of a structure.

There are marginal cases in which it is not obvious whether a dwelling has been removed from the stock. A dwelling may be left vacant for a considerable period of time. There may be doubt as to whether eventually it will be torn down, or, perhaps after renovation, occupied once more. It may not be easy to say at exactly what point a unit ceases to be part of the effective housing supply. Such doubts have arisen for some dwelling units involved in this survey which interviewers found vacant. As will be discussed in the next section, these marginal cases are especially likely to be found in the low-price parts of the rental market.

One important category of people who move into a housing unit and leave no vacancy are newly married couples who lived with their respective parents up to the time of their marriage. If the parents continue to occupy their homes, there will be no vacancy into which anyone can move. The same type of situation may exist when the people left behind after the move are not the parents of the movers out. For example, several unmarried young people may share an apartment. If one moves out, no dwelling unit is left vacant. (There may be a vacant *place* in the apartment into which another young person may move, but in this investigation such partial vacancies have not been traced.) A divorce may leave one person still living in the unit formerly occupied by a couple. Another important possibility is that new entrants into the housing market may leave behind, not a housing unit, but a vacancy in the institutional population. For example, they may have been living in a college dormitory, or on an army post. Again, they may have been living outside the United States. All of these situations have in common the fact that no vacant housing unit is left in the market.

In this type of discussion it is obviously necessary to define the borders of the market. We have defined the market in which we are interested as geographically bounded by the borders of the conterminous United States. We have also restricted the market to housing units as the Census defines the term, to the exclusion, for example, of the institutional population.

What is the actual relative importance of these different reasons for the ending of sequences of moves? An estimate can be made from the survey, but there are difficulties. For many sequences information is incomplete. Sometimes people refuse to be interviewed; sometimes a dwelling is found to be vacant; and sometimes an address cannot be found, or cannot be reached without prohibitive expense. At each position in a sequence there is a chance of failure to obtain information. Efforts to reduce the number of sequences for which information is incomplete have been made. The reasons for the endings of sequences whose ends are known have been tabulated in Table 1.

By far the most important reason why sequences end is that the last dwelling unit is still occupied by someone. Fully 63 percent of the ends are due to that reason. Forty-seven percent are still occupied by the parents of the

TABLE 1

WHY SEQUENCES OF MOVES END

(Percentage distribution of reasons,

sequences whose ends are known)

| Reason for End[a] | All Sequences | Sequences of Two or More Positions |
|---|---|---|
| Removed from the stock of housing | 20 | 18 |
| Purposely demolished (or about to be) | 8 | 8 |
| Converted to non-residential use | 3 | 3 |
| Remodeled to become part of larger dwelling unit | 4 | 4 |
| Destroyed by storm or fire | 1 | 1 |
| Seasonally vacant (has become a seasonal residence) | 4 | 2 |
| Still occupied by someone | 63 | 63 |
| Parents still live there | 47[b] | 46[b] |
| Other relatives still live there | 14 | 14 |
| Roommates still live there | 2 | 3 |
| Space vacated not a dwelling unit or not in the U.S. (includes people who left the army or some other institution) | 17 | 19 |
| Total | 100 | 100 |
| Number of sequences | 756 | 507 |

[a]Excludes sequences which end with a vacant dwelling and other sequences for which information is incomplete.

[b]Includes 6 for whom it is not known who the occupants are.

people who moved out. Other relatives are also fairly important, accounting for about 14 percent of all known ends of chains. Only about 2 percent left roommates still in possession of their old home.

About 20 percent of the sequences end because a vacated unit has been removed from the stock of housing. Demolition accounts for less than half of the removals from the stock, to be exact, only about 8 percent of the ends. About 4 percent are remodeled to become part of a larger dwelling unit, while an additional 4 percent are seasonally vacant, that is, they have been converted to seasonal residences. Conversions to non-residential use account for only 3 percent of the ends, and destruction by fire, storm or other natural catastrophe for only 1 percent.

Seventeen percent of the sequences end because the space vacated was not a dwelling unit in the housing market. This category includes sequences which end with people who (1) left the army or (2) some other institution, such as college or university housing, as well as those (3) who migrated to the United States. These three groups are of roughly equal importance.

The reader will note that Table 1 is based on 756 sequences which came to definite, logical conclusions. An additional 51 sequences ended in long vacancies, that is, the dwellings were observed to be vacant both in the fall of 1966 and in the third wave of interviews in 1967 without evidence of intermediate occupancy. (This count of 51 excludes 14 dwellings which were vacant in both years but are known to have been occupied in the interval.) If, as seems probable, these 51 dwellings which had been vacant for a year were never again used as residences, the estimate in Table 1 that 20 percent of all sequences end in removals from stock should be adjusted upward. If all 51 are regarded as removals from stock, then the adjusted estimate is that 27 percent of sequences end in this manner.

The second column of Table 1 shows the distribution of "reasons for end" for the sequences which are at least two positions long. The distribution is not very different from that for all sequences. This similarity suggests the possibility that sequences with varied starting points may come to similar ends.

This account of the reasons why sequences of moves come to an end would be more satisfactory if direct comparisons could be made between sequences which begin with new construction and the sequences with other starting points such as the attrition of the population through deaths. Adequate data are not available. An attempt to make the most of what information is available will be reported in Chapter IV.

## C. The Length of Sequences of Moves

One of the most basic questions which can be asked about the sequences of moves is simply, how long are they? This question is of interest for several reasons. If one asks how many moves will be generated by the construction of a certain number of new homes, then he is merely asking, how long will be the chains of moves generated by this new construction? If, for example, the sequences turned out to be extremely short, there would be little possibility of very much housing "filtering down" to lower income classes.

Accordingly, adjusted estimates of the length of sequences have been prepared. The essential idea behind the procedure is to estimate the "loss rate" from position to position in the sequences on the basis of those sequences whose disposition is known at each position. It is assumed that the same proportion of the other sequences continue as of the sequences whose disposition is known.

We shall proceed by presenting the results at which we have arrived, and then returning to explain in some detail the reasoning which lies behind these results. We have estimated, for different positions in the sequences of moves, the proportion of sequences which end at that position, and the proportion which continue. The "loss rate" at position one is estimated at 23.8 percent. That is, 23.8 percent of the sequences include only the new housing, implying that 23.8 percent of those who moved into the new quarters left no vacancy for subsequent occupancy by another family.

The loss rate is not the same from position to position. Our best estimate of the average loss rate at each position is as follows:

| Position | Estimated Loss Rate |
|---|---|
| One | 23.8% |
| Two | 27.3 |
| Three | 32.8 |
| Four | 29.6 |
| Five or higher | 30.5 |

In this tabulation the loss rate for "five or higher" is an average of the observed rates for positions five through thirteen. (For details see Appendix Tables E-8 and E-9.)

The increase after the first position is reasonable. People are unlikely to move into any new dwelling from a home in such poor condition that it will be torn down. Young couples are less likely to start out in a new home than in a less expensive dwelling that has been in existence for some time. Stability in the mortality rate after position three is also reasonable. By that time the series have gone far enough from the new dwelling unit so that the effect of starting at that unit has been dissipated.

These average loss rates, of course, imply a certain average length for the complete sequences. The implications are developed in Table 2, which assumes an initial 1000 new units and applies these loss rates, thus generating a distribution of sequences by length. Since a total of 3545 moves are made, the average length works out to 3.5 positions.[3]

---

[3] We may note that, by implication, 3545 interviews should have been taken instead of the actual 3039 if there had been no interviewing failures. Thus, the response rate was 3039/3545, or 85.7 percent.

TABLE 2

NUMBER OF SEQUENCES WHICH THEORETICALLY SURVIVE TO INDICATED
POSITIONS, FROM AN INITIAL 1000 NEW HOMES,
BASED ON ESTIMATED LOSS RATES

| Position | Number at This Position | Estimated Loss Rates* | Loss |
|---|---|---|---|
| One | 1000 | 23.8 | 238 |
| Two | 762 | 27.3 | 208 |
| Three | 554 | 32.8 | 182 |
| Four | 372 | 30.1 | 112 |
| Five | 260 | | 78 |
| Six | 182 | | 55 |
| Seven | 127 | | 38 |
| Eight | 89 | | 27 |
| Nine | 62 | | 19 |
| Ten | 43 | | 13 |
| Eleven | 30 | | 9 |
| Twelve | 21 | | 6 |
| Thirteen | 15 | | 5 |
| Fourteen | 10 | | 3 |
| Fifteen | 7 | | 2 |
| Sixteen | 5 | | 2 |
| Seventeen | 3 | | 1 |
| Eighteen | 2 | | 1 |
| Nineteen | 1 | | a |
| Total | 3545 | | 999 |

*
Based on observed rates for positions one, two, and three
respectively.  Later positions taken at 30.1, based on
average for the remaining positions.

a
Less than one.

It would have been much simpler to estimate the average length of sequences simply by taking the total number of interviews in the study and dividing by the number of initial new dwelling units. This simple procedure, however, would have been biassed in the direction of underestimating the average length of the sequences.

The essential problem is that the longer a sequence, the more chances there are for the sequence to end with an interviewing failure rather than a logical conclusion. At each position in the sequence there is a chance that the address will be inaccessible, that the interview will be refused, that the home will be temporarily vacant, that the project's deadline for interviewing will be reached, or that something else will prevent the interviewer from obtaining the required information. Since the risk of failure arises at each position, the probability of incomplete information for the sequence as a whole depends on the number of positions. If the probability of a success in obtaining an interview is p for any position, the probability for the sequence will be $p^n$, where n is the actual number of dwellings in the sequence. For example, if the probability of success at any position is .9, for a complete sequence of two positions the probability is $(.9)^2 = .81$; for a sequence of three positions, $(.9)^3 = .729$.

Accordingly, as noted above, special efforts were made in this project to reduce the non-response rate. If circumstances permitted (for instance, if the interviewer had not already discovered that the address given was incorrect or perhaps out of range of our national interviewing staff) interviewers were asked to go back and try again on the interviews where they had failed, once after 6 months had elapsed and then again 6 months later. In cases where a personal interview would be impossible, unless the sequence had ended with an outright refusal, a telephone interview was attempted or a mail questionnaire, depending on the information available. Thus, there were three waves of interviews taken in this study. Such efforts, however, served to control rather than to eliminate the bias.

In the estimation of loss rates it was found useful to distinguish three broad categories of situations. In the first, information was complete as a result of successful completion of the interviewing. It was known, for example, that one particular sequence continued from position two to position three, while another sequence ended at position two.

The second category includes situations in which there was an interviewing failure, in the sense that an interview which should have been completed was not completed, yet sufficient information was obtained so that it is known whether the sequence continued. The interviewer might obtain the address, go to the dwelling unit, talk to the people living there, but be refused an interview. Or the interviewer might learn from neighbors, landlord, or some other source that the dwelling is occupied, but be unable to contact the occupant. In another type of situation, the interviewer may learn that the dwelling had been occupied in the period between the second and the third waves, even though it was vacant at the time of the third wave. In these situations it is known that the sequence of moves continued at least to include this position. Someone quite definitely moved into the vacancy which was created by the previous move.

Note the difference between such a situation and the third, complete lack of information. One can fail even to obtain an address. The person who moved out of an address might simply refuse to tell the interviewer about it. One might obtain the address and be unable to locate it. He might find no proof that this address exists or ever existed.

Once the facts are at hand as to what happened in the field, there is no special problem about how to treat any of the above situations. There may be a difficulty, however, when the interviewer reports that a dwelling is vacant. There may be no interviewing failure – the interviewer has reported correctly what the facts are – but it is not obvious whether in the future the vacancy will be occupied or will be removed from the housing supply. The resulting margin of uncertainty was the basic reason for the renewed effort in the field in July and August 1967, after the initial waves of interviewing in the summer and fall of 1966. In those situations where a dwelling which had been found vacant in 1966 was still vacant in 1967, it is assumed that the dwelling will be removed from the housing supply. (This assumption, of course, does not apply if there is evidence of occupancy at any time in the interval. Under those circumstances, the sequence continues.) There will be some situations in which this assumption will be wrong since some of these dwellings will be occupied. It is further assumed that those (few) dwellings found vacant in the third wave which had been vacant less than a year all will eventually be occupied. This assumption undoubtedly introduces some error in the compensating direction. If the dwelling was vacant in the second wave and, for some reason, no report was obtained in the third wave, the sequence is assigned to the "no information" category.

Thus, an element of judgment entered the final decisions as to the treatment of these marginal decisions. The resulting range of uncertainty in the final estimate is not large. Calculations made after the second wave of interviews yielded an estimate of an average of 3.7 positions per sequence. Similar calculations made after the third wave lead to the estimate of 3.5. These estimates agree closely enough to be reassuring.

*D. Does the Length of a Sequence Depend on the Value of the New Home?*

To this stage the analysis of the length of series of moves has assumed that the series are all alike. Yet the new homes which initiate the series are by no means homogeneous. Are there differences in length of sequence depending on the value of the new home, and on whether it is owned or rented? Behind this question lies another: when high income people build expensive homes are they thereby initiating long sequences of moves so that low income people ultimately benefit, or do the sequences thus initiated end before anything happens which benefits poor people?

In attempting to answer these questions we shall use two sets of estimates. The first set is based on the number of dwellings in each sequence for which there was no interviewing failure; the second, on complex estimates of loss rates such as those undertaken for the sample as a whole. The first set of calculations suffers from the limitation already discussed, that short sequences are more likely to be followed to their logical conclusion without interviewing failure. It has the advantage, however, that there is no need to make complex assumptions and imputations to deal with problems of incomplete information. At least, we know the length and other characteristics of these sequences. We can readily examine in detail the relation between the characteristics of the initial dwelling and the length of the sequences.

We note, first, as shown in Appendix Table E-10, that the mean length for all sequences about which information is complete is 2.6, which we know to be too short owing to the bias resulting from the fact that short sequences are easier to complete. This bias, however, should operate regardless of the economic value of the initial property. The *relative* lengths of sequences with different beginnings are the focus of interest.

There is a large difference in length of sequence between series begun by rented as contrasted to owner-occupied homes. The series which begin with a rented unit are much more likely to end quickly. The mean length of sequences which begin with owner-occupied homes is one full position longer than for rental homes (3.1 versus 2.1). This result is reasonable since new apartments are more likely than new houses to be occupied by young couples who leave no vacant former home. (For a discussion of who moves into new apartments see Chapter III.)

GRAPH 3

MEAN LENGTH OF SEQUENCES FOR WHICH INFORMATION IS COMPLETE,
SEQUENCES BEGINNING WITH OWNER-OCCUPIED HOMES

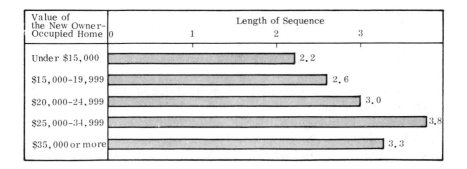

GRAPH 4

MEAN LENGTH OF SEQUENCES FOR WHICH INFORMATION IS COMPLETE,
SEQUENCES BEGINNING WITH RENTED HOMES

| Monthly Rent of the New Dwelling | Length of Sequence | | | |
|---|---|---|---|---|
| | 0 | 1 | 2 | 3 |
| Under $100 | 1.7 | | | |
| $100–124 | 1.9 | | | |
| $125–149 | 2.0 | | | |
| $150–199 | 2.7 | | | |
| $200 or more | 3.2 | | | |

We are especially concerned with the relation between the price of the new dwelling at position one and the length of the sequence. The main findings are shown in Graphs 3 and 4.

As shown in Graph 3, within the category of sequences which begin with owner-occupied homes the value of the new home seems to make a considerable difference in the number of dwellings in the sequence. Houses valued over $35,000 initiate sequences only fractionally longer than the average (3.3 versus 3.1). The inexpensive houses, however, initiate short sequences. Houses valued under $15,000 initiate sequences about 0.9 positions shorter than the average (2.2 versus 3.1).

Further, sequences which begin with new homes of low rental value are especially likely to be short. As shown in Graph 4, for those which begin with a unit renting for under $100, the average length of sequence is about 0.4 positions less than the average for all sequences beginning with rented units (1.7 versus 2.1). Sequences beginning with a unit renting for $200 or more are about 1.0 positions longer than the average (3.2 versus 2.1).

The first set of estimates thus indicate that the length of a sequence does indeed depend on the value of the new home. High priced houses initiate considerably longer sequences than inexpensive new homes.

If the results had been otherwise, the analysis could have stopped at this point. If the sequences begun by expensive homes had proven to be short, we could have concluded that poor people are unlikely to benefit from the construction of new homes. As it is, we are led to consider these long sequences more carefully. We must consider just how much longer these sequences are, taking into account the troublesome problem of interviewer failure. The second set of estimates, accordingly, is based on a more complex procedure. Essentially, calculations similar to those shown in Table 2 were repeated for each of four types of sequences classified according to the characteristic of the new dwelling unit at the start of each sequence. The details are shown in Appendix Table E-11. The main results are as follows:

| Characteristics of the New Dwelling | Average Length of Sequence |
|---|---|
| Rented | |
| Less than $150 per month | 2.4 |
| $150 or more | 3.9 |
| Owner-occupied | |
| Valued less than $25,000 | 3.8 |
| Valued $25,000 or more | 4.5 |

These estimates of length, as expected, are longer than the averages of the first set of calculations. The sequences which begin with rented units valued below $150 per month are 1.5 positions shorter than those which begin with units valued at $150 per month or more. Sequences which begin with expensive houses, valued at $25,000 or more, average 0.7 positions longer than those which begin with houses valued below $25,000. We shall make further use of our estimates of the length of sequences in the next chapter.

*E. The Location within a Metropolitan Area of Successive Dwellings*

We have stressed in the discussion to this point, and will emphasize in Chapter III, the economic level of the occupants of houses at successive positions in the sequences of moves. An alternative approach is to put the issue in terms of geography: will a policy of encouraging new construction in suburban areas have an indirect impact upon crowded conditions in the center of a city? From this point of view it is appropriate to ask concerning the dwellings at successive positions, where are they located within the metropolitan areas? Where are the new dwellings situated? Is there a tendency for the sequences to develop inward toward the center of the city as they become longer?

These questions must be examined within one metropolitan area at a time. The city of Detroit was chosen as a convenient locality for investigation. The approximate distance from a fixed point in the center of the city to each of the new dwellings was measured. In addition, the distances from that fixed central point to all the successive dwellings in each sequence were calculated (unless the sequence left the metropolitan area entirely).

Sixty-one sequences began in Detroit and remained within the city for at least one further position. For these sequences, the mean distance from the center to the new dwelling was 18.2 miles, and the median distance also 18.2 miles. Only four new dwellings in the Detroit sample, less than 7 percent, were located ten or fewer miles from the center of the city. The mean distance from the center to the last dwelling in each of these sequences was 12.7 miles, and the median 10.9. Twenty-nine of these final dwellings, almost half, were located ten or fewer miles from the center of the city. To summarize:

|                                        | Position in Sequence | |
| Miles from the Center of Detroit | First | Last |
| --- | --- | --- |
| Mean distance | 18.2 | 12.7 |
| Median distance | 18.2 | 10.9 |
| Number of dwellings | 61 | 61 |

The tendency for sequences to move closer to the center as they get longer can be seen even more clearly if the distances from the city center are examined for the dwellings arranged by position. The median declines sharply after the first position, from 18.2 to 12.3 miles, and continues to decline slowly for positions two and beyond, as shown in Graph 5. The mean declines more gradually than the median after the first position, from 18.2 to 14.6. It falls again to 12.2 at position three and continues to decline slowly, except for a small rise at position five. At position one, 6 percent of the dwellings are within ten miles of the center, 31 percent at position two, 50 percent at position three, 53 percent at position four, and 54 percent at positions five and above. The details are shown in Appendix Table E-12.

GRAPH 5

MEDIAN DISTANCE FROM THE CENTER OF DETROIT

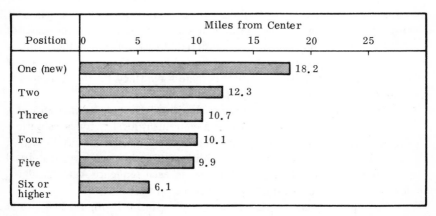

We may conclude that, as expected, most of the new construction in Detroit is taking place on the edges of the metropolitan area. People who wish to better their housing situation in the city move further out in order to do so. New construction on the periphery does have indirect consequences for crowding in the central city. Since these findings are broadly consistent with expectations, we have not prepared similar calculations for other cities.

# 3
# The Characteristics Of Successive Families In The Sequences

TO this point in the consideration of the succession of moves begun by new construction we have been concerned with the characteristics of the housing units involved, with only incidental references to the characteristics of the occupants. We now turn to that topic. The first section of this chapter considers in some detail the characteristics of the occupants of the new homes. The question is considered, who moved into new apartments and who, into new single family houses? The second section is concerned with changes in tenure, and the third, with the stage in the family life cycle of the families who move, and the degree of crowding. Most changes in stage in the life cycle involve changes in the number of people in the family and, hence, changes in the degree of crowding, unless there are associated changes in the dwelling unit occupied.

The last two sections of the chapter are concerned with the position in the successions of moves of families of different social status: the fourth section considers families of different income; the last, families of different race. These two sections are directly related to the question of the efficiency of the filtering process.

## A. The Occupants of the New Homes

In any cross-section survey taken at one period of time there is always the question, would the results have been different at some earlier date? Will they be different if the study is repeated in the future? For definitive answers to such questions it is usually necessary to repeat a survey. Yet, it is possible at least to consider the question, what was going on at the time of the survey which was unusual and also relevant to the results? For this project the answer is obvious: during the early 1960's there was a remarkable increase in the construction of apartments in this country. For housing units in structures containing three or more units the peak years were 1963 and 1964, with over 550,000 apartments started in 1963. These units represented about 34 percent of all housing units started. In 1966 total starts were lower, but the 411,000 apartments started continued to represent a third of all starts.[1] For metropolitan areas the percentage of new housing units which are apartments is undoubtedly higher. In this project it is 42 percent.

We have seen in the previous chapter that the sequences of moves begun by new apartments are shorter than those begun by new owner-occupied homes. We would like to know, then, whether the mix of types of new dwelling is likely to continue to be 42 percent apartments. We would also like to know whether the tendency for sequences begun by apartments to be short may reasonably be expected to continue.

We shall not be able to come to definite conclusions on these points, but we shall offer tentative opinions. There is also considerable interest in the reasons for the apartment boom as a phenomenon in its own right. It has been suggested by some observers that the large numbers of apartments built in recent years reflect a shift in preferences away from single family homes toward multiple family structures. Economists who have studied the housing market have been more inclined to interpret the demand for housing in terms of factors of such as income and the demographic composition of the population. The data collected for the present study offer an opportunity to analyze these interpretations. Is the demand for new apartments symptomatic of a basic shift in preferences from single family homes to apartments? If there is such a shift, it should be possible to observe individual families who move from single family homes to new apartments.

*Who shifted from single family homes to new apartments?* The present sample is representative of all families who moved into new apartments in metropolitan areas of more than 200,000 population. What proportion of these people lived in single family homes before they occupied the new apartments? The answer is as follows:

| Type of Dwelling Where Family Lived | Percent of Families Who Moved Into New Apartments |
|---|---|
| Single family | 36 |
| Other | 64 |
| Total | 100 |
| Number of families | 484 |

[1]U.S. Bureau of the Census, **Construction Reports, Housing Starts**, April 1967.

Thus, 64 percent were not shifting from single family homes to apartments. Although 36 percent of those who moved to new apartments did come from single family homes, it by no means follows that 36 percent were giving up single family homes for apartments. Many were young people who had been living with their parents in their parents' homes, which the parents continued to occupy. To understand these moves it is necessary to examine what happened to the single family homes after the moves to the apartments. The disposition of these homes was as follows:

| Detailed Disposition of Former Homes | Percent of Those Who Moved From Single Family Homes to New Apartments |
|---|---|
| Still occupied by some of the former residents | 53 |
| Parents still live there | 41 |
| Other relatives still live there | 11 |
| Roomates still live there | 1 |
| Dwellings no longer used | 6 |
| Dwellings no longer exist | 2 |
| Other (seasonally vacant, not dwellings in the universe) | 4 |
| Dwellings made available for a new family | 41 |
| Total | 100 |
| Number of families | 174 |

Just over half of the former homes (53 percent) were still occupied by part of the same family (or group of people living together) that had been there before some members left for a new apartment. Of all who moved from a single family home to an apartment, only about 41 percent actually freed the single family home so that a new family could move in. Another way to look at the matter is to note that of all movers to new apartments only 15 percent both moved out of a single family home and left that home free for occupancy by another family.

Were these 15 percent making the change because of a shift in preferences or because of a change in their stage in the life cycle? The data permit explicit joint consideration of stage in the family life cycle of movers to new apartments and the disposition of their former homes (Table 3). As just noted, people who moved from single family homes to apartments and freed a dwelling unit are 14 or 15 percent of all movers to new apartments. Few of them (only 1 percent) are young couples with no children. The largest group (7 percent) are older couples without children and older single people. These moves are understandable as part of the process of aging without any need to assume a shift in preferences. When people in the older age groups move into an

TABLE 3

FORMER HOUSING ARRANGEMENT OF MOVERS INTO NEW APARTMENTS,
SHOWING STAGE IN THE FAMILY LIFE CYCLE[a]

(Percentage distribution of movers into new apartments)

| Whether a Dwelling Unit was Freed by Movers into New Apartments | All | Stage in Family Life Cycle | | | | | | | | |
|---|---|---|---|---|---|---|---|---|---|---|
| | | Young, Unmarried | Young, Married, No Children | Age of Youngest Child | | | Older, Married, No Children | Older, Unmarried | Unmarried, with Children | Stage Not Ascertained |
| | | | | Under 5 | 5-14 | 15-17 | | | | |
| Freed no dwelling unit | 33 | 10 | 12 | 5 | 1 | * | 2 | 2 | 1 | * |
| Freed a dwelling unit | 67 | 10 | 13 | 10 | 4 | 1 | 16 | 10 | 2 | 1 |
| Single family house | 14 | * | 1 | 2 | 2 | 1 | 5 | 2 | 1 | * |
| 2-4 family house | 13 | 1 | 4 | 2 | 1 | * | 2 | 2 | 1 | * |
| Apartment | 38 | 8 | 8 | 6 | 1 | * | 8 | 6 | * | 1 |
| Other | 2 | 1 | * | * | * | * | 1 | * | * | * |
| All | 100 | 20 | 25 | 15 | 5 | 1 | 18 | 12 | 3 | 1 |
| Number of movers | 484 | | | | | | | | | |

*Less than one-half of one percent.

[a]The term "young" means under 45; "older" means 45 or older. The term "unmarried" includes those never married, and those widowed, separated (temporarily or otherwise) or divorced. The term "no children" means no children under 18 living at home.

apartment, unless they move from another apartment they are likely to free a single family dwelling for another family to occupy. In contrast, the young people who move into new apartments rarely leave a single family dwelling unit free for some other family to occupy. In fact, of all movers into new apartments only about 1 percent are young people who free a single family home, in spite of the fact that young people without children account for 45 percent of the moves into new apartments.

To summarize the main facts about moves into new apartments, we may divide the movers into three groups, "young," counting as "young" all young, single people and young couples; people with children; and "old" people, counting as "old" all those in later stages of the life cycle. Then the "young" account for more than four out of ten moves into new apartments (45 percent). They hardly ever move out of single family homes to apartments and free the single family home. Those with children account for over two out of ten moves to apartments (24 percent). They occasionally free a single family home. The "old" account for the remaining three out of ten new apartments (30 percent). They fairly often are leaving a single family home free for another family: 7 percent of all moves to new apartments are of this type.

*Income, life cycle, and the choice between a new apartment and a new house:* There are two factors generally agreed to be of fundamental importance in analysis of the demand for housing, family income and the demographic characteristics of the population, here summarized in the form of stage in the family life cycle. The following presentation will show, first, the effect of income and life cycle separately, and second, the joint effects of the two. The basic dependent variable under consideration is the choice between a new apartment and a new single family house for people who moved into one or the other. Note the change in strategy. To this point in the discussion we have proceeded by close consideration of the circumstances of people who move into new apartments. We now compare movers into apartments with movers into single family homes.

Inertia is important in the housing market. Many people tend to be reluctant to move, and stay on in a dwelling after it has ceased to be appropriate for their circumstances. Those who have just moved into a new home have overcome this inertia. Can we then say that they are "in equilibrium" in the sense that they have adjusted their housing to their financial position, their needs and preferences, and the existing market? Some may plan to move again soon, for example, those who have just moved into an area for the first time. Yet it seems reasonable to suppose that most of these recent movers into new homes are closer to an equilibrium adjustment than a cross-section of the population at large.

Family income, considered as a single variable, is strongly related to people's choice of type of new home (Appendix Table E-13). Of those with incomes under $2,000 who moved into a new home, 9 percent moved into a single family home and 91 percent into a unit in a multiple family structure. Of those with incomes over $15,000 who moved into a new dwelling unit, 65 percent moved into a single family home and only 35 percent into a multiple family structure.

There is reason to doubt, however, that the simple cross-section relation of Appendix Table E-13 correctly estimates the relation between income and housing type for movers into new homes. As incomes rise in the future, a different relation or set of relations to choice of housing may apply. Income and stage in the life cycle both must be considered. The effect of life cycle on the percent of those moving into a new home who move into a single family home is as follows:

| Stage in Life Cycle | Percent of Movers into New Homes in Each Stage in the Family Life Cycle Who Move into New Single Family Homes |
|---|---|
| Young, single | 6 |
| Young, married, no children | 27 |
| Married, youngest child under 5 | 70 |
| Married, youngest child 5-18 | 84 |
| Over 45, married, no children under 18 | 38 |
| Over 45, not now married (single, widowed, divorced) | 15 |
| All families | 51 |

Only 6 percent of young, single people who move into a new home move into a new single family house, compared to 84 percent of families with school age children. It hardly needs emphasis that the difference between 6 percent and 84 percent is as large a difference as one often observes in cross-section data.

What the problem clearly requires is joint consideration of the effects of income and life cycle, and an attempt to estimate their joint effect may be found in Graph 6 (see also Appendix Table E-14). There is definite evidence of an income effect, and the effect is in the direction of an association of higher income with choice of single family homes rather than apartments.

Most families with children clearly prefer to avoid apartments and move out of them when they can afford to do so. The effect of income on the choice is very strong for those with children under 5. For those older families whose youngest child is 5 to 18 the effect of current income is much less, essentially because even the lower income families by this time in their lives have managed to acquire the assets to become home owners.

GRAPH 6

PERCENT OF THOSE MOVING INTO A NEW DWELLING WHO MOVED
INTO AN APARTMENT

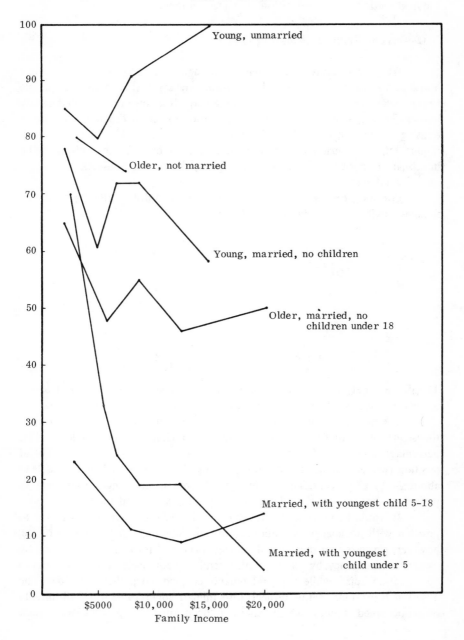

Young, unmarried

Older, not married

Young, married, no children

Older, married, no
children under 18

Married, with youngest child 5-18

Married, with youngest
child under 5

Family Income

We have, then, the result that in general high incomes are associated with living in single family homes. Why, then, the boom in the demand for new apartments in a period of rising incomes? We shall find a possible explanation in the next section in a consideration of changes in tenure.

## B. Owners and Renters: Changes in Tenure

Whether a family owns or rents its home is related to whether it lives in a house or an apartment, but it is by no means the same. It is possible for people to own apartments, and, of course, people may either own or rent single family houses. Tenure is relevant for the interpretation of recent developments in the housing market proposed above. Tenure is also a matter of basic concern in any inquiry into the housing of the poor since they are by definition unlikely to be in a financial position to buy such an expensive asset as a house except on the most favorable terms.

Consider, once more, the new dwellings. The distribution by tenure of families moving into new homes is as follows:

| Tenure (after move) | Percent of New Homes |
|---------------------|----------------------|
| Own                 | 53                   |
| Rent                | 46                   |
| Neither             | 1                    |
| Total               | 100                  |
| Number of interviews | 1144                |

The division between owners and renters in the new homes at the start of the sequences, thus, was very nearly equal, with a few more owners than renters.

The percentage of owners shifts from one position to the next position in the sequence of moves, however, as shown in Graph 7 (and Table 5). This percentage falls from 53 at position one (the new housing units) to 39 at position two, and 30 at position three. At positions four and above it is stable at about 24 to 27 percent. The percentages of renters, accordingly, rises from 46 percent to the range of 70 to 75 percent at positions four and above.

It would be possible theoretically to observe such a relation of tenure to position with no change in tenure for any dwelling unit. Common experience, however, suggests that dwellings do change back and forth from occupancy by owners to occupancy by renters, with a tendency for single family dwellings to be owner-occupied while new and tenant-occupied when they are older. The observed transitions in this project are summarized in Table 4. Of all initially owner-occupied homes which changed occupants, 17 percent were next

GRAPH 7

OWNERS AS A PERCENT OF ALL OCCUPANTS FOR HOUSING UNITS
AT DIFFERENT POSITIONS

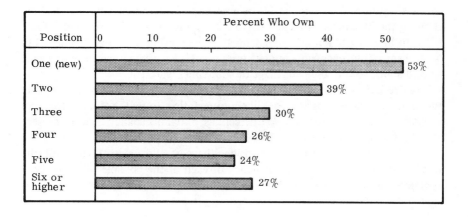

TABLE 4

TRENDS IN TENURE, SAME DWELLING[a]

(Percentage distribution of dwellings)

| Tenure of Present Occupants | All | Tenure of Former Occupants | |
|---|---|---|---|
| | | Owned | Rented |
| Own | 33 | 83 | 8 |
| Rent | 67 | 17 | 92 |
| Total | 100 | 100 | 100 |
| Number of dwellings | 1812 | 595 | 1217 |

[a]Excludes 85 dwellings which either before or after the
shift in occupants fell into the category "neither owned
nor rented."

occupied by renters. Of renter occupied dwellings, 8 percent were next occupied by owners.

To place in the context of the total market the trends in tenure just described, we may compare the distribution of movers-in by tenure shown above to a distribution of all families in the population by tenure. Such a distribution, showing the breakdown by income groups, appears in detail in Appendix Table E-15. In brief, of all families in metropolitan areas 60 percent own, compared to 53 percent of the occupants of new dwellings. Hence, there is evidence of a shift toward an increase in the percentage of all families who rent.

We have here what seems to be a paradox. Incomes are rising. People in the upper income groups are more likely to own than to rent. Yet, new dwellings in large metro areas show a *higher* percentage rental occupancy than the average for all housing in all metro areas in the country in early 1966.

To resolve the paradox, consider the past and present tenure of the families at each position. The frequency of each of the possible shifts has been estimated, and is shown in Table 5. Of all families moving into new homes

TABLE 5

PAST AND PRESENT TENURE STATUS BY POSITION OF THE FAMILY IN THE SEQUENCE

(Percentage distribution of families)

| Past and Present Tenure Status of Family | All | Position in the Sequence of Moves | | | | | | |
|---|---|---|---|---|---|---|---|---|
| | | 1 | 2 | 3 | 4 | 5 | 6 | 7 or higher |
| Now own | 40 | 53 | 39 | 30 | 26 | 24 | 27 | 27 |
| Formerly owned | 18 | 26 | 17 | 11 | 10 | 7 | 7 | 15 |
| Formerly rented | 18 | 23 | 18 | 16 | 13 | 12 | 13 | 11 |
| Formerly other[a] | 4 | 4 | 4 | 3 | 3 | 5 | 8 | 1 |
| Now rent | 58 | 46 | 60 | 67 | 72 | 73 | 71 | 72 |
| Formerly owned | 6 | 6 | 7 | 5 | 6 | 5 | 6 | 5 |
| Formerly rented | 34 | 25 | 37 | 38 | 44 | 43 | 44 | 43 |
| Formerly other[a] | 18 | 15 | 16 | 24 | 22 | 25 | 21 | 24 |
| Now other[a] | 2 | 1 | 1 | 3 | 2 | 3 | 2 | 1 |
| Formerly owned | * | * | * | * | * | 1 | * | * |
| Formerly rented | 1 | * | * | 1 | 1 | 1 | 1 | 1 |
| Formerly other[a] | 1 | 1 | 1 | 2 | 1 | 1 | 1 | * |
| Total | 100 | 100 | 100 | 100 | 100 | 100 | 100 | 100 |
| Number of families | 3039 | 1146 | 786 | 495 | 270 | 156 | 86 | 100 |

*Less than one-half of one percent.

[a]"Other" includes those who neither own nor rent and those whose status was not ascertained.

(families at position 1 in the sequence), 23 percent were shifting from renting to owning, and 6 percent, from owning to renting. Note that this table refers to families. The trends in tenure for the same dwelling, discussed in the preceding section, are another matter. It is quite possible for families to change back and forth from owning to renting with no change in the percentage of dwellings which are owner-occupied, and, indeed, with no change in tenure for any individual dwellings. Yet in the aggregate the number of families who own must match the number of homes which are owner-occupied.

Consider, however, the important group who before the move studied were neither owners nor renters. Of all families studied, 23 percent were formerly neither owners nor renters. The great bulk of these families, 18 percent of the 23 percent, were formerly in the "other" category and became renters after the move. Included among them are young people who formerly lived with their parents or were in the armed forces, college dormitories, and the like.

Apart from them, 6 percent shifted from owning to renting and 18 percent from renting to owning, for a net shift of 12 percent to owning. Only by taking the "others" into account is it possible to reconcile the trends in tenure status by family with the trends in tenure by dwelling. The basic phenomenon is a shift toward more people maintaining independent dwellings.

The transition from renting to owning is of interest as a phenomenon in its own right. Many people aspire to own their homes, and one of the objectives of public policies toward housing is to facilitate home ownership. It might be supposed that the people who buy *new* homes would be those who had been owners for some time and had accumulated an equity. The data partially support this reasoning. Such families account for about half the families who bought *new* homes whereas they account for only about one-third of all those who bought at the third or later positions.

Another way of looking at these results is to note that the 53 percent who own at position one include 23 percent who are becoming owners after being renters and 4 percent who formerly neither owned nor rented. Thus, about half of the people moving into new homes are becoming owners as they do so. Yet, the ratio of new owners to all owners is even higher at the later positions. At the second position, new owners are 22 percent while all owners are 39 percent of occupants. At the third position, new owners are 19 percent compared to all owners who comprise 30 percent — that is, new owners are six owners out of ten.

One might also suppose that the reverse transition, from owning to renting, would be likely to involve new apartments. People who have enjoyed their own home, one might argue, would be most likely to desire and be able to afford a new apartment. The data do not support this argument. The proportion of movers who are shifting from owning to renting is about equally high at each position in the sequence.

We propose the conclusion that the increased demand for new apartments in the period studied was not the result of a basic shift in popular preferences away from single family homes. The explanation must be sought elsewhere, in such factors as the changing proportion of the population at different stages in the family life cycle and the effect of rising incomes on people's ability to maintain separate dwellings.

What are the possible implications for the length of sequences of moves in the future? We suggest that the time of the survey was a period of rising demand for separate dwellings for people who earlier had not been able to maintain homes of their own. There was an increase in what is sometimes called the "headship rate," ie. in the proportion of adults who are heads of their own units. Apartments to meet this demand were scarce. Under such conditions it is reasonable to find that sequences initiated by new apartments are short. We would expect that, when the headship rate stabilizes, as it must eventually, the sequences initiated by new apartments will become longer. We would also expect that the percentage of new units which are apartments would eventually decline, with a corresponding tendency for the average length of sequences of moves begun by new construction to become longer.

## C. Crowding and Stage in the Family Life Cycle

One of the basic processes of adjustment in the housing market is the process by which the number of people in a family is adjusted to the number of rooms in a dwelling unit. If this adjustment were the only consideration in the matching of people to housing, there would be systematic changes in the number of rooms occupied by a family as the family passed through each stage in the family life cycle. The number of rooms would increase with the transition from single to married and increase further with the birth of children. The number of rooms occupied would decrease as the children left home one by one, and decrease further with the death of one of the partners, until finally the family ceased to exist. In fact, people do seem to increase the number of rooms they occupy more or less as their families grow, but they often keep rooms needed only for occasional visits after the children have grown up and left home.

The succession of families who occupy the same dwelling unit can be examined using this study to determine the association between the stage in the life cycle or the age of those who move out and those who move in. (This comparison, of course, is possible only when somebody did move in: eg. if the dwelling was destroyed there is no family who moved in). If the preceding sketch of the transition is correct, then ordinarily those who move in should be younger than those who move out. Even if the whole population is considered, movers-in need not be and are not identical with movers-out. There are always young people starting out who appear as having "moved in" but not as having "moved out"; and older people who move out (by dying or going to a nursing home or the like).

If people are classified into a system of eight stages in the life cycle, then the comparison may be summarized as follows:

|  | Percent |
|---|---|
| People who moved out are at a later stage than those who moved in | 41 |
| People who moved out are at the same stage as those who moved in | 31 |
| People who moved out are younger than those who moved in | 28 |
| Total | 100 |
| Number of families | 1792 |

As expected, it is common for those who move out to be at a later stage in the family life cycle than those who move in. But fully 28 percent of moves involve the reverse situation: those who move out are at an earlier stage. The details of the classification and the relationship are shown in Appendix Table E-16. The cells in Appendix Table E-16 which fit the idea of a succession of occupants of dwellings based on the succession of stages in the life cycle are fairly well populated — but so are some of the cells which do not fit. For example, when couples with young children move out of a dwelling, 10 percent of the time the people who move in are older couples with no children under 18.

Essentially the same pattern emerges when the age of the head of the family is used to classify the family rather than the stage in the family life cycle (Appendix Table E-17) for example, when a family with head 18-24 moves out and is succeeded by another family, 45 percent of the time it is succeeded by a family with head also 18-24, as expected, but 55 percent of the time it is succeeded by a family with head 25 or over.

We are led to suggest two tentative interpretations. First, although the succession of occupants of the same dwelling does on the average involve a transfer from older to younger families — as it must — this transfer accounts for only a comparatively small part of the activity in the housing market in the sequences begun by new construction. Second, the successions of moves begun by new construction may not be typical of all moves in this respect. Sequences begun by a death, for example, no doubt would be different.

Even when attention is restricted to sequences begun by new construction, the transfer between stages in the life cycle becomes very apparent when entire sequences of moves are considered. As shown in the following tabulation, about half (49 percent) of the sequences involving two or more families show a progression in the expected direction, and only 27 percent a reversal.

| Change in Life Cycle[a] | Percent |
|---|---|
| Families in new dwellings are at a later stage than those at the last position | 49 |
| Families in new dwellings are at the same stage as those at the last position | 24 |
| Families in new dwellings are at an earlier stage than those at the last position | 27 |
| Total | 100 |
| Number of sequences of moves involving two or more families | 713 |

[a]Based on a classification of the life cycle into eight stages.

Similarly, about half (54 percent) show that the family in the new home is older than the last family in the sequence.

| Change in Age of Head of Family[a] | Percent |
|---|---|
| Heads of families in new homes are older | 54 |
| Older by three age brackets or more | 13 |
| Older by two age brackets | 16 |
| Older by one age bracket | 25 |
| No difference in age | 24 |
| Heads of families at last position are older | 22 |
| Older by one age bracket | 11 |
| Older by two age brackets | 7 |
| Older by three or more age brackets | 4 |
| Total | 100 |
| Number of sequences of moves involving two or more families | 713 |

[a]Based on comparisons of classifications of heads of families in a bracket code which uses ten year intervals except for an initial interval from 18-24, inclusive, of seven years. The fact that the median falls in the category "older by one age bracket" implies that the head of the family in the new dwelling is about ten years older.

Only 22 percent are characterized by a younger family in the new home than in the last dwelling in the series.

What are the implications for crowding? Older families are likely to be smaller. It is not surprising, therefore, that the number of people per family is on the average smaller in the new homes than in the homes at the completion of the sequences. Forty-six percent of the sequences show fewer people in the families in the new homes, and only 29 percent the reverse. The distribution follows:

| Change in Family Size | Percent |
|---|---|
| Families in new homes have fewer people | 46 |
| Three fewer people (or more) | 12 |
| Two fewer people | 16 |
| One fewer person | 18 |
| No change | 25 |
| Families in new homes have more people | 29 |
| One more person | 13 |
| Two more people | 9 |
| Three additional people (or more) | 7 |
| Total | 100 |
| Number of sequences of moves involving two or more families | 713 |

It is also not surprising to find that the new homes tend to have more rooms than those at the last positions in the sequences. It was noted above that the dwelling at the last position is likely to be rented, and to be an apartment. In fact, the following distribution shows 64 percent of the new homes have more rooms than the homes at the last positions in the respective sequences of moves.

| Change in Number of Rooms | Percent |
|---|---|
| New homes have more rooms than those at last position | 64 |
| Four additional rooms (or more) | 13 |
| Three more rooms | 12 |
| Two more rooms | 20 |
| One more room | 19 |
| New homes have same number of rooms as those at the last position | 19 |
| New homes have fewer rooms than those at the last position | 17 |
| One fewer room | 8 |
| Two fewer rooms | 5 |
| Three fewer rooms (or more) | 4 |
| Total | 100 |
| Number of sequences of moves | 713 |

As a consequence, the number of people per room is usually less in the new dwellings than in the last dwellings in the sequences. The number of people per room is smaller in the new dwelling in 52 percent of the sequences; it is greater in 35 percent. The full distribution is as follows:

| Change in People Per Room | Percent |
|---|---|
| Crowding less in the new dwellings | 52 |
|     By 0.6 people per room or more | 10 |
|     By 0.5 people per room | 6 |
|     By 0.4 people per room | 7 |
|     By 0.3 people per room | 7 |
|     By 0.2 people per room | 13 |
|     By 0.1 people per room | 9 |
| | |
| Crowding the same at first and last positions | 13 |
| | |
| Crowding greater in the new dwellings | 35 |
|     By 0.1 people per room | 10 |
|     By 0.2 people per room | 10 |
|     By 0.3 people per room | 5 |
|     By 0.4 people per room | 5 |
|     By 0.5 people per room | 3 |
|     By 0.6 people per room | 2 |
| | |
| Total | 100 |
| | |
| Number of sequences of moves | 713 |

That there should usually be less crowding in the new dwelling is as expected; if anything, it is surprising to find that greater crowding at the start of the sequence is as common as it seems to be.

### D. Poverty Levels, Income and Education

The economic position of the successive families in the sequences of moves begun by new construction is a matter of interest to anyone concerned with the indirect effects of new construction on the housing market as a whole. Table 6 shows the income distribution for families at each position separately. For the moment, let us take as a rough measure of poverty a family income below $3000 at the time of the survey, 1966. Then only about 6 percent of the families who move into new homes are poor (Graph 8). At the second position the proportion who are poor is also small, 8 percent. At later positions about 15 percent are poor. It is especially interesting to note the approximate stability of the income distribution of movers for positions 3 and above. The distributions are virtually identical, given the sampling error of the estimates.

TABLE 6

FAMILY INCOME BY POSITION

(Percentage distribution of families)

|  | All Positions | Position in the Sequence of Moves | | | | | |
|---|---|---|---|---|---|---|---|
| Family Income |  | 1 | 2 | 3 | 4 | 5 | 6 or higher |
| Less than $3000 | 9 | 5 | 7 | 14 | 14 | 16 | 12 |
| Less than $2000 | 5 | 3 | 3 | 8 | 8 | 9 | 6 |
| $2000-2999 | 4 | 2 | 4 | 6 | 6 | 7 | 6 |
| $3000-5999 | 27 | 17 | 32 | 31 | 30 | 40 | 29 |
| $3000-3999 | 7 | 5 | 7 | 10 | 8 | 12 | 6 |
| $4000-4999 | 8 | 4 | 9 | 9 | 8 | 13 | 11 |
| $5000-5999 | 12 | 8 | 16 | 12 | 14 | 15 | 12 |
| $6000 or more | 64 | 78 | 61 | 55 | 56 | 44 | 59 |
| $6000-7499 | 15 | 13 | 16 | 18 | 20 | 13 | 18 |
| $7500-9999 | 20 | 23 | 18 | 18 | 18 | 11 | 20 |
| $10,000-14,999 | 20 | 28 | 18 | 13 | 14 | 16 | 17 |
| $15,000 or more | 9 | 14 | 9 | 6 | 4 | 4 | 4 |
| Total | 100 | 100 | 100 | 100 | 100 | 100 | 100 |
| Number of families | 2705[a] | 1034 | 700 | 434 | 236 | 139 | 162 |

[a]Excludes families for whom income was not ascertained.

GRAPH 8

PERCENT OF FAMILIES WITH INCOME LESS THAN $3000 AT EACH POSITION

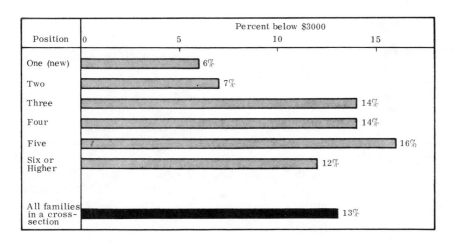

For purposes of comparison, income distributions for all families in metropolitan areas in the United States for 1965 are shown in Table 7. A closer comparison can be made with the income of all families in the 17 metropolitan areas selected for this study. It is instructive that about 13 percent of all families in these metropolitan areas have incomes below $3000. Thus, from position 3 onwards poor people form a slightly higher percentage of those who benefit from sequences of moves than they do of the population of metropolitan areas.

At the first position, people with income of $6000 or more are overrepresented. They form 78 percent of those who move into new housing in contrast to 68 percent of the population of these metropolitan areas. High income people are not overrepresented in the complete sequences. Those with incomes of $10,000 and above make up 38 percent of the population but only 29 percent of all families in the sequences of moves. People in the income range $3000–5999, however, are overrepresented at every position after the first. They represent about 20 percent of the population of metropolitan areas, but they are 30 percent or more of the families at every dwelling after position one. Thus, the sequences of moves do extend down into the middle and lower income groups.

It may be urged that family income is a crude measure of economic welfare. A leading objection is that income does not take into account the number of people in a family, while expenditures do depend on the number of people. To take the number of people into account we have used a scale which, in effect, is based on the proposition that a family needs $1000 plus $500 per individual to avoid poverty. The classification is as follows:

| | |
|---|---|
| Poor | $Y < \$1000 + \$500\,n$ |
| Affluent | $Y > 3(\$1000 + \$500\,n)$ |
| Middle class | $\$1000 + \$500\,n < Y < 3(\$1000 + \$500\,n)$ |

The "n" represents the number of people in the family. Note that those who have an income of three times the amount needed to avoid being "poor" are defined as "affluent."

The adoption of the above standard of poverty instead of $3000 per annum has the effect of reducing from 6 to 4 percent the estimate of the percent of those who move into new homes who are poor, as the following tabulation shows:

TABLE 7

A COMPARISON OF INCOME DISTRIBUTIONS FOR ALL FAMILIES IN THE UNITED STATES
AND ALL POSITIONS IN THE SEQUENCES OF MOVES

(Percentage distributions of families)

| Family Income | United States as a Whole, 1965[a] | | | The 17 Metropolitan Areas Sampled in the Sequences of Moves | Sequences of Moves, All Families[b] |
|---|---|---|---|---|---|
| | All Areas | Outside Metropolitan Areas | All Metropolitan Areas | | |
| Less than $3000 | 20 | 26 | 17 | 13 | 9 |
| Less than $2000 | 11 | 15 | 9 | 7 | 5 |
| $2000-2999 | 9 | 11 | 8 | 6 | 4 |
| $3000-5999 | 23 | 29 | 21 | 19 | 27 |
| $3000-3999 | 8 | 11 | 7 | 7 | 7 |
| $4000-4999 | 7 | 8 | 7 | 6 | 8 |
| $5000-5999 | 8 | 10 | 7 | 6 | 12 |
| $6000 or more | 57 | 45 | 62 | 68 | 64 |
| $6000-7499 | 13 | 13 | 13 | 13 | 15 |
| $7500-9999 | 17 | 15 | 18 | 17 | 20 |
| $10,000-14,999 | 17 | 11 | 20 | 23 | 20 |
| $15,000 or more | 10 | 6 | 11 | 15 | 9 |
| Total | 100 | 100 | 100 | 100 | 100 |
| Number of families | 2419 | 698 | 1721 | 1050 | 2705 |

[a]Source: 1966 Survey of Consumer Finances.

[b]Interviews were taken in 1966 but asked for 1965 income.

| Position Number | Percent Who Are Poor | Total Number of Families[a] |
|---|---|---|
| One | 4 | 1034 |
| Two | 6 | 703 |
| Three | 13 | 435 |
| Four | 12 | 238 |
| Five | 17 | 139 |
| Six | 11 | 73 |
| Seven or higher | 12 | 89 |

[a]Excludes families for whom Poverty-Affluence Level was not ascertained.

For positions 3 and above it remains true that approximately 13 to 14 percent of the families are classified as poor. Other definitions of poverty, of course, may be proposed. We doubt that their use would change the conclusion that poor families are substantially underrepresented at positions 1 and 2 but comprise at least the same proportion of movers at positions 3 and above that they represent of the population of metropolitan areas.

We may combine these results concerning the proportion of movers-in who are poor with our estimate of the length of sequences of moves from the preceding chapter. The result is expressed as an estimate of the total number of poor people who are able to move as a result of the construction of an initial 1000 new homes. The calculations are shown in Table 8.

It is estimated there that there will be a total of 3545 families who move, implying an average length of sequence of 3.545. It is estimated that poor families will be .04 of all families at position one, .06 at position two, and .139 thereafter. On this basis a total of about 333 poor families will be included in the sequences begun by the 1000 new homes.

This estimate is obviously sensitive to the definition of poverty. If more or fewer people are defined as poor, the number of poor people estimated as included in the sequences will necessarily vary. The reader can experiment with the use of different cutting points on the income distribution on the basis of Table 6. Two facts will remain true, whatever cutting point is adopted: there are about 1800 families at positions three, four and above and the lower end of the income distribution for the families at these positions is about the same as the lower end of the income distribution for all families in metropolitan areas. Hence, if 20 percent of the population are defined as poor, roughly 20 percent

TABLE 8

ESTIMATE OF THE NUMBER OF POOR FAMILIES WHO ARE
INCLUDED IN THE SEQUENCES OF MOVES RESULTING
FROM AN INITIAL 1000 NEW HOMES

| Position | Estimated Number of Families at Each Position, from Initial 1000 New Homes | Estimated Proportion of the Families at Each Position Who Are "Poor" | Estimated Number of "Poor" Families at Each Position |
|---|---|---|---|
| One | 1000 | .04 | 40 |
| Two | 762 | .06 | 46 |
| Three | 554 | .139[b] | 77 |
| Four | 372 | | 52 |
| Five | 260 | | 36 |
| Six | 182 | | 25 |
| Seven | 127 | | 18 |
| Eight | 89 | | 12 |
| Nine | 62 | | 9 |
| Ten | 43 | | 6 |
| Eleven | 30 | | 4 |
| Twelve | 21 | | 3 |
| Thirteen | 15 | | 2 |
| Fourteen | 10 | | 1 |
| Fifteen | 7 | | 1 |
| Sixteen | 5 | | 1 |
| Seventeen | 3 | | a |
| Eighteen | 2 | | a |
| Nineteen | 1 | | a |
| Total | 3545 | | 333 |

[a] Less than one.

[b] The estimate of .139 "poor" is a weighted average of the observed proportion who are "poor" at positions 3 and above.

of these 1800 families will be poor; if 10 percent of the population are defined as poor, roughly 10 percent of the 1800 families will be poor. Poor families will be represented at positions three and above in approximately the same proportion which they represent of the population.

We are now in a position to consider the effect on the number of poor families in a sequence of characteristics of the new home. The following tabulation is based on calculations of length of sequence based on estimated loss rates in the manner outlined in the previous chapter:

| | Characteristics of the New Dwelling | | | |
| | Rented | | Owner-Occupied | |
| Characteristics of the sequences[a] | Under $150 Per Month | $150 or More Per Month | Value under $25,000 | Value $25,000 or More |
|---|---|---|---|---|
| Average length of sequence | 2.40 | 3.90 | 3.83 | 4.50 |
| Number of poor families who move per 1000 new dwellings | 270 | 252 | 366 | 323 |

[a]Calculated on the assumption that sequences in which the last observed dwelling was vacant for less than a year will continue, while those vacant for a year or more will be removed from the supply of housing.

These findings are also shown in Graph 9.

GRAPH 9

AVERAGE LENGTH OF SEQUENCES, BASED ON ADJUSTED ESTIMATES

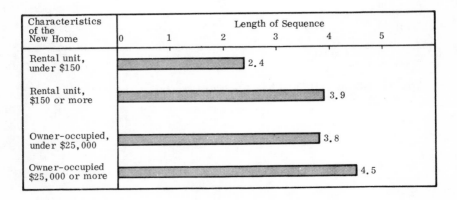

The number of poor families who benefit is greatest when the new dwelling is owner-occupied with value under $25,000. This finding is the result of the greater length of the sequences which begin with owner-occupied homes. We have already suggested that the short average length of sequences which begin with rental units may be the result of the conditions in the housing market at the time of the study, that is, of the rising demand for apartments.

These estimates depend on two sets of probabilities, the probability that a sequence will survive from position to position, and the probability that, if it does survive, the people who move in will be poor. We present these basic estimates in graphic form in Graph 10. Each section of Graph 10 begins with a

GRAPH 10

ESTIMATED NUMBER OF POOR PEOPLE AND PEOPLE NOT POOR
WHO MOVE PER 1000 NEW HOMES

Part A.  Sequences Begun by New Homes Renting Under $150

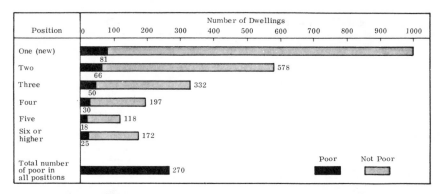

Part B.  Sequences Begun by New Homes Renting for $150 or More

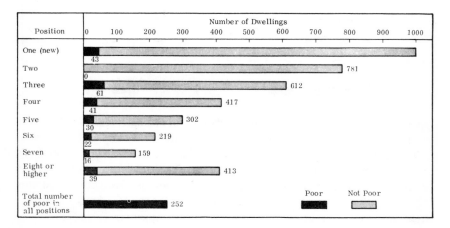

GRAPH 10 -- Continued

Part C.   Sequences Begun by New Homes Valued at Under $25,000

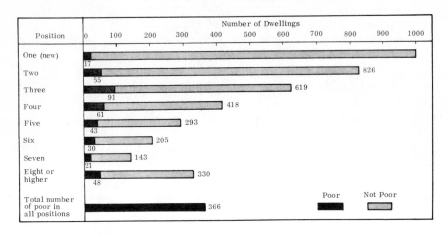

Part D.   Sequences Begun by New Homes Valued at $25,000 or More

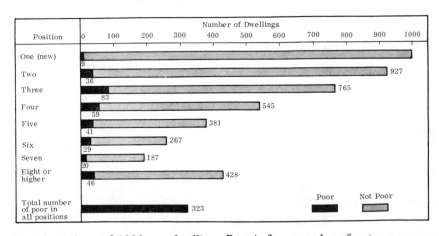

hypothetical set of 1000 new dwellings. Part A, for example, refers to sequences begun by new homes renting for under $150. Of these sequences, 578 survive to position two, 332 to position three, and so forth. At each of these positions some of the people will be poor, as indicated by the shading of part of the bar at that position. The total number of poor in all positions has been cumulated; it is 270 for sequences begun by 1000 new homes renting for under $150. (This total corresponds to that in the text table above. See also Appendix Table E-11.)

The results, of course, are subject to sampling error. We present them as our best estimates, but it should be understood that the calculations have been carried out to three figures for purposes of accounting accuracy rather than because the data are accurate to the third figure.

We may approach the filtering process in another way by considering the income of the people who move out of a specific, individual dwelling and comparing it with the income of those who move in. In this study information on family income was obtained only in class intervals, so that what can be done is to compare the income brackets of the families in question. (For the nine intervals used see Table 7 above.) We have as many observations as we have dwellings which were occupied by two families. As shown in Table 9, 55 percent of the dwellings were occupied by people with lower incomes after the move and

TABLE 9

DIFFERENCES IN INCOME LEVEL, SUCCESSIVE OCCUPANTS OF THE SAME DWELLING

(Percentage distribution of dwellings)

| Income of Movers-Out Compared with Movers-In | All Dwellings Which were Occupied by Two Families | Position of the Dwelling in the Sequence of Moves | | | | |
|---|---|---|---|---|---|---|
| | | 2[a] | 3 | 4 | 5 | 6 or Higher |
| Movers-in have lower income | 55 | 61 | 56 | 43 | 56 | 46 |
| Within the same bracket | 20 | 19 | 18 | 25 | 16 | 20 |
| Movers-in have higher income | 25 | 20 | 26 | 32 | 28 | 34 |
| Total | 100 | 100 | 100 | 100 | 100 | 100 |
| Number of dwellings | 1511 | 630 | 394 | 218 | 122 | 147 |

[a]The dwelling at position 2 is the first in any sequence for which it is possible to compare the income of those who moved out with the income of those who moved in.

25 percent by people with higher incomes. The general tendency, thus, is in the expected direction, but there are substantial numbers of shifts in the opposite direction.

There is some tendency for this income comparison to depend on position number. At position two, about six out of ten movers-in have lower incomes, as expected. At later position numbers, only about half of the movers-in have lower incomes. The proportion of movers-in with higher incomes than those they replace increases from about two out of ten (for position two) to three out of ten at positions three and above.

Income tends to change systematically as people pass through their working lives. Education, however, does not usually change after people once leave school. Education also may be taken as a proxy for social status. Accordingly, it may be of interest to examine the succession of people of different education levels in the same dwellings. It is surprising how little correlation there is between the education levels of the heads of the successive occupants. Using a classification of education into eight levels the education of the head of the family who moved in may be compared to that of his predecessor as follows (see also Appendix Table E-18):

| Education of the Head of Family Who Moved in Compared to that of the Head of the Family Who Moved Out | Percent |
| --- | --- |
| Higher by two positions or more | 20 |
| Higher by one position | 12 |
| Same | 28 |
| Lower by one position | 14 |
| Lower by two positions or more | 26 |
| Total | 100 |

There is a considerable shift of housing toward those of lower education — but there is almost as large a shift in the opposite direction. For example, 17 percent of movers-out were college graduates (without graduate work). Of those who moved in after them, four out of ten had no more than a high school education. There is less stratification of the housing market by social status than one might have supposed.

### E. Negroes in the Succession of Moves

While the results of the preceding section indicate that housing shifts easily from families of one socio-economic level to those of another, these findings imply nothing about shifts between races, which must be examined directly. In this study the sample of non-whites other than Negroes is too small for analysis: only Negroes can be considered. The question of how many Negroes benefit from new construction may be divided into three questions: What proportion of new dwellings are initially occupied by Negroes? What proportion of sequences of moves which start with one race at some position change to another race, especially from white to Negro? If a sequence of moves involves Negroes, how long is that sequence?

Of all new homes in metropolitan areas in the study, 5 percent are occupied by Negroes. This percentage is less than would be expected simply on the basis of the proportion of the population who are Negroes. Exactly what should be taken as the population estimate for purposes of comparison, however, is not a simple question. According to the 1966 Survey of Consumer Finances, 9.3 percent of all families in the 17 metropolitan areas in question are Negro. That estimate is probably too low. Of the total population of the U.S. in all metropolitan areas in 1966 the Census Bureau estimates 12.7 percent were non-white, implying about 11 percent Negro.[1] It is not clear that Negroes are 11 percent of all families. The age distributions by race differ, and a smaller percentage of Negroes than whites are married, age being taken into account. If the standard of comparison is taken as about 10 percent Negro, 5 percent implies that Negroes receive roughly half of a proportionate share of new housing. As long as that situation continues Negroes, more than whites, must look elsewhere for improved housing.

It is well known that Negroes have lower incomes than whites, and, hence, it is hardly surprising that Negroes do not share in new housing in proportion to their numbers. We now ask a more difficult question: are Negroes underrepresented among occupants of new homes more than one would expect simply on the basis of their income?

To answer this question we have first estimated the percentage of families at each income level who are Negro in a cross-section of the 17 metropolitan areas under study. This estimate could not be made from the present survey but was obtained from the 1966 Survey of Consumer Finances. The results appear as column B of Table 10, and are more or less as expected. Negroes make up large proportions of low income groups and small proportions of high income groups.

We then apply these proportions to the observed number of families in each income group who live in the new homes at position one. Negroes, we argue, if they make up .14 of all families below $2000 might be expected to make up .14 of all such families in new homes. Summing over income groups we obtain a total expected proportion of Negro families at position one. On the basis of the Negro income distribution, thus, we expect 8.43 percent Negro. We observe 5.1 percent Negro. We conclude that Negroes make up .61 of the number of families in new housing that we would expect on the basis of their income.

Is this estimate biased? As noted above, some Negroes are missed in cross-section surveys such as the Survey of Consumer Finances. Any error in this direction tends to lead to an understatement of the proportion of Negroes in column B and, hence, to an understatement of the total expected number of

---

[1]Current Population Survey, Series P-20, No. 171, April 30, 1968, p. 7.

TABLE 10

ESTIMATE OF THE NUMBER OF NEW HOMES WHICH NEGROES MIGHT BE EXPECTED
TO OCCUPY ON THE BASIS OF THEIR INCOMES

| | A | B | AxB |
|---|---|---|---|
| | | Proportion of Families in a Cross-Section of the 17 Metropolitan Areas | |
| 1965 Total Family Income | All Families at Position One | Who are Negro, within Each Income Group* | Cross Product |
| Less than $2000 | 3.2 | .14 | .448 |
| $2000-2999 | 2.5 | .20 | .500 |
| $3000-3999 | 4.7 | .17 | .799 |
| $4000-4999 | 4.6 | .14 | .644 |
| $5000-5999 | 7.9 | .19 | 1.501 |
| $6000-7499 | 12.7 | .07 | .889 |
| $7500-9999 | 23.0 | .08 | 1.840 |
| $10,000-14,999 | 27.9 | .06 | 1.674 |
| $15,000 or more | 13.5 | .01 | .135 |
| All | 100.0 | .09 | 8.430 |

Number of families        1034

Number of Negroes in new homes = 58

Total number of people in new homes = 1128

Percentage Negro:   58/1128 = 5.14

Expected percentage Negro = 8.43

Ratio:  $\frac{\text{Observed}}{\text{Expected}} = \frac{5.14}{8.43} = .610$

---

*Special tabulation from the 1966 Survey of Consumer Finances.

Negroes. It seems unlikely that there is any substantial offsetting tendency to miss new homes occupied by Negroes in this survey. (The list of building permits for new dwellings is probably reasonably complete.) If there is a net bias, then, it is probably in the direction of overestimating the proportion. Negroes actually occupy something less than .61 of the new homes that one would expect them to occupy on the basis of their income.

It must be recognized that Negroes are at a financial disadvantage in the housing market because of their lack of accumulated reserves as well as their low incomes. The fact that Negroes occupy only .61 of the new homes that one would expect on the basis of their incomes is the combined result of discrimination in the housing market and Negroes' low average assets. In early 1962 the average net worth for the population as a whole was estimated at $14,600 in the Survey of Consumer Finances. The average net worth of families successfully interviewed in that survey was estimated as follows:

Mean Net Worth (1962)[a]

| Age | Negro | White |
|---|---|---|
| 18-24 | $ 100 | $ 2,000 |
| 25-34 | 1,400 | 7,800 |
| 35-44 | 3,700 | 15,000 |
| 45-54 | 3,800 | 24,000 |
| 55-64 | 4,400 | 31,300 |
| 65 or older | 3,500 | 22,300 |
| All | $2,900 | $15,900 |

[a]Does not include pension accumulations or insurance reserves.

Thus, average net worth for whites is more than five times average net worth for Negroes. It is obvious that a Negro couple seeking to buy a new home is likely to have difficulty raising a large down payment. They themselves may not have the needed capital, and they may not be able to obtain it by such expedients as borrowing from their parents. It would be theoretically possible to attempt to separate the combined effect of all the financial disadvantages under which many Negroes labor from the effect of direct racial discrimination in the housing market. We have not attempted such a calculation.

When Negroes do move into new housing, they are more likely to move into new apartment houses than into new single family homes, as the following tabulation shows:

| Type of Home | All | White | Negro |
|---|---|---|---|
| Single family house | 51 | 52 | 33 |
| 2-4 family house | 7 | 6 | 10 |
| Apartment | 42 | 42 | 57 |
| Other | * | * | * |
| Total | 100 | 100 | 100 |
| Number of homes | 1138 | 1056 | 58 |

*Less than one-half of one percent.

More than half (57 percent) of the Negroes who move into a new dwelling moved into an apartment compared to 42 percent of the whites. Many of these new apartments must be located in urban neighborhoods in which Negroes already are living.

It is possible to make very approximate estimates of the rents paid by Negroes as well as whites who moved into new apartments. The median rent for Negroes is estimated at $95 compared to $130 for whites. (The full distributions of rent are shown in Appendix Table E-19.)

Very few Negroes moved into new single family homes. For those who did, the median price was $19,700, compared to $23,100 for whites (see also Appendix Table E-20).

While these last estimates for Negroes are subject to large sampling errors, they fit together into a pattern which corresponds to expectations. Negroes are unlikely to move into a new home. If they do, they tend to move into an apartment rather than a house, and the apartment tends to be low-priced. If they do acquire a new house, they tend to pay a somewhat lower price than the typical white occupants of new houses though they may, because of various restrictions, pay more for an equivalent house than whites.

It is less obvious what to expect about the incomes of the Negroes who move into new homes. One might suppose that only the few prosperous Negroes would be able to move into such homes, and that, therefore, the incomes of these families would be fairly high. In fact, of the comparatively few Negroes who did move into new units, over half (56 percent) had incomes below $6000. Of the whites who moved into new units, only about 20 percent had incomes below $6000 (Appendix Table E-21).

We turn to the consideration of the total number of Negroes who occupy positions in sequences of moves. The percentage of Negro families to all families in the sequences of moves studied is 7.0. Since, as already noted, Negroes make up roughly 10 percent of all families in the metropolitan areas studied, they are clearly underrepresented. They appear in the sequences roughly 70 percent as often as they should on the basis of their numbers alone.

To what extent is this underrepresentation due to the fact that Negro incomes are lower? We already have a clue to the answer to this question since we know that the income distribution of all families in sequences of moves is not very different from the income distribution of all families in the areas involved. Poor people participate in the sequences. The level of Negro incomes, therefore, would not lead one to expect that they would be unable to participate. The question can be answered more precisely on the basis of an investigation for complete sequences carried out in the same manner as the calculations already described for new homes. The calculations are shown in Table 11. On the basis of their incomes we would expect Negroes to occupy about 10 percent of the positions in the sequences of moves. The observed result, 7.0 percent, is 70

TABLE 11

ESTIMATE OF THE NUMBER OF POSITIONS IN SEQUENCES OF MOVES WHICH NEGROES
MIGHT BE EXPECTED TO OCCUPY ON THE BASIS OF THEIR INCOMES

| 1965 Total Family Income | A<br>All Families - All Positions in Sequences | B<br>Proportion of Families in a Cross-Section of the 17 Metropolitan Areas Who are Negro, within Each Income Group* | AxB<br>Cross Product |
|---|---|---|---|
| Less than $2000 | 4.8 | .14 | .672 |
| $2000-2999 | 4.4 | .20 | .880 |
| $3000-3999 | 6.9 | .17 | 1.173 |
| $4000-4999 | 7.7 | .14 | 1.078 |
| $5000-5999 | 11.7 | .19 | 2.223 |
| $6000-7499 | 15.2 | .07 | 1.064 |
| $7500-9999 | 19.7 | .08 | 1.576 |
| $10,000-14,999 | 20.5 | .06 | 1.230 |
| $15,000 or more | 9.1 | .01 | .091 |
| All | 100.0 | .09 | 9.987 |

Number of families        2705

Number of Negroes in new homes = 58

Number of Negroes at positions 2, 3, etc. = 146

Total number of Negroes in the sequences = 204

Total number of families = 2930

Percentage Negro:   204/2930 = 6.962

Ratio: $\frac{\text{Observed}}{\text{Expected}} = \frac{6.962}{9.987} = .70$

---

*Special tabulation from the 1966 Survey of Consumer Finances

percent of the expected result. This percentage, then, is a measure of the disadvantage of Negroes in the housing market, income being taken into account.

Is the underrepresentation of Negroes in sequences of moves in some sense due to a tendency of Negroes not to move at all? To this question, the answer is negative since on the average Negroes move *more* than whites. The percentage of Negro families who move to a new address in a year is 20.8 as against 18.0 for whites.[2]

Negroes can benefit from a sequence of moves beginning with new construction either if the new dwelling unit is occupied by a Negro family or if there occurs in the sequence of moves a transition from white to Negro occupancy. Such transitions are comparatively rare. As Table 12 indicates, 3 percent of the dwellings occupied by two families actually shifted from white to Negro. The opposite shift, from Negro to white, was very rare, only 1 percent of all moves. How should these percentages be regarded? Assuming that Negroes comprise 10 percent of all families, it is possible to define the expected number of changes in race on the assumption that the race of the first occupant has nothing to do with the race of the second. On that basis, 10 percent of the dwellings vacated by whites would be occupied by Negroes. About 9 percent of all dwellings, that is, 10 percent of the 90 percent that were white, would shift from white to Negro at each link after the first, and, by similar reasoning, about 9 percent would shift the other way, Negro to white. The observed percentages are very much smaller. The transition from white to Negro occurs about a third as often as it would if race had nothing to do with housing.

It may be urged that transitions from white to Negro occupancy are rare for sequences of moves which begin with new construction because new construction is expensive, and Negro incomes are low. Hence, one might expect more such transitions at positions later in the sequences, say, at positions three and beyond. As shown in Table 12, the percentage of dwellings at which this transition occurs never rises over 4 percent.

Although these transitions are uncommon in sequences of moves which begin with new construction, 51 are available in our sample and are worth describing. In Table 13 tenure is considered. The moves involving change of race from white to Negro are compared to all moves, to all moves involving whites who move in, and to all moves involving Negroes who move in. It appears that Negroes who negotiate this change are more likely to have been home owners before the move than other movers-in. Some of these Negroes were renters, but virtually none of them formerly had "other" tenure arrangements. In other words, young Negro couples are more likely to make this transition by purchasing a home than by renting. After the move 44 percent of them were owners, compared to 34 percent of all whites who moved and about 23 percent of all Negroes who moved.

There remains the question on the relative length of sequences by race. Table 14 shows by race the disposition of the previous home of people who move. The difference between the races is striking. Thirty-three percent of all moves by Negroes leave someone still occupying the former home, compared to

[2]*Current Population Reports*, Series P-20, No. 163, March 27, 1967.

TABLE 12

CHANGES IN RACE[a]

(Percentage distribution of dwellings from sequences
of two or more positions)

| Change in Race | All | 2 | 3 | 4 | 5 | 6 or Higher |
|---|---|---|---|---|---|---|
| | | | Position of Housing Unit | | | |
| No change | 94 | 96 | 93 | 93 | 91 | 93 |
| Negro to white | 1 | * | 1 | 1 | * | 1 |
| Negro to other | * | * | * | * | 1 | 1 |
| Other to white | 1 | * | * | 1 | * | * |
| White to other | 1 | 1 | 2 | 1 | 3 | 2 |
| Other to Negro | * | * | * | 1 | 1 | 1 |
| White to Negro | 3 | 3 | 4 | 3 | 4 | 2 |
| Total | 100 | 100 | 100 | 100 | 100 | 100 |
| Number of dwellings | 1753 | 745 | 455 | 245 | 143 | 165 |

*Less than one-half of one percent.

[a]Excludes mail and telephone interviews for which race
was not ascertained.

TABLE 13

CHANGE IN TENURE, DWELLINGS CHANGING FROM WHITE TO NEGRO OCCUPANCY

(Percentage distribution of dwellings)

| Change in Tenure for Dwelling Unit | All Moves | All Moves Involving Whites Who Moved In | All Moves Involving Negroes Who Moved In | Moves Involving Change, White to Negro |
|---|---|---|---|---|
| Formerly owned | 33 | 34 | 26 | 46 |
| Now owned | 27 | 28 | 21 | 41 |
| Now rented | 5 | 6 | 5 | 5 |
| Now other | 1 | * | * | * |
| Formerly rented | 65 | 65 | 73 | 54 |
| Now owned | 5 | 5 | 2 | 3 |
| Now rented | 59 | 59 | 70 | 49 |
| Now other | 1 | 1 | 1 | 2 |
| Formerly other; neither; not ascertained | 2 | 1 | 1 | * |
| Now owned | 1 | 1 | * | * |
| Now rented | 1 | * | 1 | * |
| Now other | * | * | * | * |
| Total | 100 | 100 | 100 | 100 |
| Number of dwellings | 1888 | 1578 | 140 | 57 |

*Less than one-half of one percent.

TABLE 14

DISPOSITION OF PREVIOUS HOME BY RACE

(Percentage distribution of moves for
which information is available)

| | | Race | |
| Disposition of Former Homes | All | White | Negro |
| --- | --- | --- | --- |
| Sequences continue | 69 | 71 | 49 |
| Temporarily vacant | 3 | 3 | 6 |
| Dwellings no longer exist | 4 | 4 | 8 |
| Seasonally vacant | 1 | 1 | * |
| Someone still lives there | 18 | 17 | 33 |
| Space vacated not a dwelling | 5 | 4 | 4 |
| Total | 100 | 100 | 100 |
| Number of moves | 2729 | 2428 | 183 |

*Less than one-half of one percent.

17 percent of moves by whites. It appears that Negroes are crowded, and, when a Negro family moves into a different dwelling, often some members of the group who had been living together still occupy the original dwelling. As a result, sequences of moves involving Negroes tend to end more quickly than sequences involving only whites. Any increase in the proportion of sequences of moves which involve Negroes is likely to lead to some decrease in overall average length of sequence.

We are forced to the conclusion that Negroes benefit less than whites from new construction. Negroes occupy new homes in smaller numbers than their percentage of the population or their incomes would justify. There is some shifting of dwellings from whites to Negroes as sequences of moves develop, but not enough for Negroes to benefit in proportion to their numbers.

A word of caution concerning these results is appropriate. We have not attempted to measure over-all welfare gains in this study. For example, we have not attempted to estimate whether one family benefits more than another by moving. One might argue, say, that people who were extremely crowded benefit more from moving than people who were slightly crowded. We have not attempted to make such judgments, restricting ourselves to counting who moves and who does not move. We have also left unanswered questions concerning gains and losses to people other than movers. Landlords, for example, obviously have interests in what takes place in the housing market, but these interests are beyond the scope of this project.

# 4
# Sequences Of Moves
# In The Context Of
# National Statistics

IT is the purpose of this chapter to place this investigation in the context of national statistics about the housing market. By so doing it is intended to check, as closely as may be feasible, the accuracy of the survey estimate of the average length of sequences. It is also proposed to consider the relative importance of sequences which begin with new construction and sequences with other beginnings. The concluding section considers the sequences in the light of the total number of moves made by all families in the nation in a year.

*A. Sequences of Moves and National Estimates of the Total Number of*
*Sequence Beginnings and Ends*

It will be recalled that there are two ways in which sequences of moves begin, by construction of new housing and by removal of families from the population occupying existing dwelling units. A family may be removed from the population in several ways, by death, by doubling up with another family, by entering the institutional population, or by emigration. Account must be taken of additions of housing units to the stock by means other than the construction of brand new units, especially by subdivision of existing units and by conversion of structures from seasonal occupancy or from non-residential use to year-round housing units.

There are also, it will be recalled, two basic ways in which sequences of moves end. They end with the permanent removal of a unit from the stock of year-round housing. Such removals include demolitions and other forms of physical destruction such as by fire or flood. Removals include conversions of structures to seasonal occupancy or to non-residential use. Sequences end when units are lost by combination of two or more existing units into one larger unit. Sequences of moves also end with the appearance of a new family. A family comes into existence, from this point of view, when it first occupies a housing unit. The occasion may be marriage, the setting up of an independent home by an unmarried adult, immigration, or leaving the institutional population.

A source of statistical difficulty is that while the entry or exit of a family may be the result of one of the events indicated, it does not follow automatically from the occurence of the event that a family will be added or subtracted. For example, a death will not add a unit to the available supply if the widow lives on in the home formerly occupied by two adults. A marriage will not add to the number of families seeking housing if one of the couple already occupied a housing unit of his own. The difficulty is that the available statistics about the underlying events — deaths, marriages, divorces, and the like — cannot easily be adjusted into statistics about the required number of housing units.

Since every sequence of moves must have both a beginning and an end, in one sense the number of beginnings and ends must be equal. In any given period, however, the number of beginnings and ends need not be equal since sequences which begin in one period may end in another period. Precise equality of the number of beginnings and ends of sequences also requires that each sequence have one and only one beginning, and one and only one end. There are situations, fortunately not very common, in which this requirement is not met. For example, if two people marry and move into one new apartment, to trace out the sequences of moves both of the resulting vacancies must be considered. It is approximately but not precisely true that the number of beginnings and ends should be equal.

For the nation as a whole it is possible to assemble some very rough estimates of the total number of beginnings and ends of sequences of moves. The estimates are summarized in Table 15. They refer only in part to the time period of this study.

The number of new units constructed in a year, of course, is closely related to the number of housing starts, which was about 1,500,000 in 1965. Starts in that year should be a fairly close approximation of completions in late 1965 to early 1966, the period with which this study is especially concerned.

Gross additions to stock from conversions, mergers, relocations, and other sources can be estimated only on the basis of Census data for earlier years. These data for 1956-1959 show an average annual rate of about 520,000. In the absence of current data it is assumed in Table 15 that the annual number of such additions to stock continued at this level in 1965-1966.

TABLE 15

APPROXIMATE ESTIMATES OF THE TOTAL ANNUAL NUMBER OF SEQUENCES
OF MOVES IN THE UNITED STATES, 1966
(Based on a variety of sources as indicated)

|  | Approximate Annual Rate (Housing Units) |
|---|---|
| **A. Sequence Beginnings** | |
| 1. New units (based on 1965 housing units started)[a] | 1,500,000 |
| 2. Gross additions to stock from conversion, merger, other sources (annual rate observed by Census 1956-1959 of 520,000) | 520,000 |
| 3. Units made available by death, emigration, etc.: (potential supply released by 1.6 million deaths of adults - 800,000 units)[b] | 800,000 |
| Total number of sequence beginnings | 2,820,000 |
| **B. Sequence ends** | |
| 1. Demolitions, conversions, mergers, and other withdrawals from stock (based on annual rate observed by Census 1956-1959, of 1,000,000) | 1,000,000 |
| 2. New households | |
| Marriages 1,800,000 (1965)[c] | |
| Immigration 70,000[d] | |
| Average annual increase, 1956-1959, in number of non-husband-wife families 400,000[e] | |
| Total number of new households 2,270,000 | 2,270,000 |
| Total number of sequence ends | 3,270,000 |

[a]See L. Jay Atkinson, "Long-Term Influence Affecting the Volume of New Housing Units," Survey of Current Business, Nov. 1963, Table 9.

[b]Statistical Abstract, 1966.

[c]Statistical Abstract, 1966 from Public Health Service, Vital Statistics of the U.S.

[d]Based on data from Burnham O. Campbell, Population Change and Building Cycles, Bureau of Economic and Business Research, University of Illinois, 1966. See especially pages 191-194.

[e]Atkinson, op. cit., Table 4.

The estimate of the number of units made available by death, emigration, etc. is also uncertain. The annual number of deaths of adults is about 1.6 million. It is fairly stable, tending to rise slowly. The death of two adults presumably will sooner or later free one housing unit. But the connection between deaths and vacant units is by no means direct. Indeed, during the 1950's there was an increase of about 400,000 per year in the number of family units not including both a husband and wife but occupying a housing unit. Most of these units are headed by a middle-aged or elderly single man or woman. More widows and widowers have been able to maintain separate homes as incomes have risen. The number of homes released by death is shown at 800,000 in the table only as a gross approximation. Adding these three sources of new sequences of moves gives the total shown in the table, about 2,800,000 sequence beginnings per year.

The total of 2,800,000 is highly approximate. It seems likely that the number of homes released by death has not yet reached 800,000 owing to the increasing tendency of widows to keep their homes. The number of conversions, etc., however, may well be greater than in the 1950's. The errors in these estimates, thus, appear likely to be partially offsetting. If the total is somewhere near right, then new construction accounts for roughly six out of ten of the sequence beginnings.

We turn to sequence ends. As far as removals from the stock of housing are concerned, once again there are no current national data. The best available information is based on the studies conducted by the U.S. Bureau of the Census which refer to the period 1957-1959.[1] To say the least, it seems doubtful that the rate of removals from stock remained constant from the late 1950's to 1966. Removals from stock were running at the rate of about 1 million a year during the period 1957 through 1959. The gross removal statistics have been summarized as follows:

| Gross Removals, 1957-1959 | Number of Housing Units | |
|---|---|---|
| | Three Years[a] | Annual Rate |
| Total removals | 3,035,000 | 1,018,000 |
| Demolition | 791,000 | 264,000 |
| Conversion | 294,000 | 98,000 |
| Merger | 739,000 | 246,000 |
| Other | 1,211,000 | 404,000 |

[a]Cited in Atkinson, op. cit., Table 9.

---

[1]Bureau of the Census, U.S. Census of Housing: 1960, Vol. IV. Components of Inventory Change – 1957-1959 Components. Final report, HC (IV), Part 2, No. 1

In these statistics "conversions" include all large housing units which were removed from the stock, subdivided, and later returned to the stock as smaller units. "Mergers" include smaller units which were removed from the stock and later combined into larger units and returned to the stock. The "other" category includes 500,000 units which were relocated at new sites as well as conversions to seasonal or non-residential use, and the accidents and disasters. Table 15 assumes continuation of the annual rate of 1,000,000 a year.

In Table 15 it is further assumed that new household formation may be approximated by the number of marriages plus a small adjustment for immigration. The annual increase in the number of non-husband-wife households once again is assumed to continue at the 1956-1959 level. More satisfactory treatment of these problems must await better data.

The reader will note that the number of beginnings and ends of sequences in Table 15 do not agree. The estimates shown are 2,820,000 beginnings and 3,270,000 ends. If the total of 3,270,000 is correct, then the 1,500,000 new units represent slightly less than five sequence beginnings out of ten, not six out of ten, as previously suggested.

It may be helpful to contrast the estimates of Table 15 with more familiar presentations. Atkinson, for example, presents the following summary statistics, among others, based on experience from 1950 to 1960:[2]

| Increase in households | 9.1 million | Losses | -3.0 million |
| Increase in vacancies | 2.3 million | New housing units constructed | 15.5 million |
| Increase in housing inventory | 11.4 million | Increase in inventory | 12.5 million |

Two estimates of increase in inventory which should agree actually differ by 1.1 million. For purposes of comparison with Table 15 the important point is that the statistics on households show the *net* increase, not the gross changes. It is, thus, impossible to compare the volume of housing released by death, etc., with the volume of new construction. In this respect the Atkinson paper is typical. Most of the statistical work refers to *net* new household formation.[3] The estimates implicitly or explicitly subtract out the number of households which disappear from the scene.

Furthermore, most of the statistics readily available refer to husband-wife families. Such families are formed, of course, by marriages, and there

---

[2]Atkinson, op. cit., Table 1. Above statistics on increase in households are based on Current Population Survey estimates.

[3]See, for example, Robinson Newcomb, "Forecasting Housing Units," **Dynamic Aspects of Consumer Behavior**, 1963, Foundation for Research on Human Behavior, Ann Arbor, Michigan, pp. 57-74.

are counts of the number of marriages: as already noted, about 1,800,000 per year in the United States. About one household in four, however, does not involve a husband-wife family. It may include more than one related person, or it may include only a single person. As previously stressed, it is known that the total number of such households increased dramatically from 1950-1960. That fact, however, is informative about the *net* increase rather than the gross increase in the number of households which do not include a husband-wife family.

Before abandoning aggregate statistics, however, we may attempt to extract from them some approximate idea of the relative importance of different reasons why sequences of moves come to an end, which may then be compared with what has been found to date about the ends of sequences in this research, keeping in mind that the survey refers to large metropolitan areas. The preliminary survey estimate based on sequences satisfactorily followed to their logical conclusions is that one fourth of sequences begun by new construction end in a demolition or permanent withdrawal from stock. (See page 12.) (Where possible, when a unit was divided, survey procedure was to consider both units as part of the sequence to be followed.) As shown above, demolitions were estimated at 264,000 a year by the Census in the period 1956-1969. "Other" removals (losses from accidents and disasters, condemnation, conversion to non-residential use) are also permanent withdrawals from stock − except for 166,000 units relocated. Total permanent removals were about 667,000 per year. If we add the above rough estimate of 2,270,000 new households formed, the total of new households plus permanent removals is 2,937,000. Of that total the permanent withdrawals are 23 percent.

Should we expect the one fourth and 23 percent to agree? Only if we expect sequences of moves begun by new construction to end in demolition as often as sequences otherwise initiated. Since sequences begun by new construction start, as it were, at the top of the market, while sequences begun by death, etc., do not, it is reasonable that comparatively a smaller proportion of the former should end with a demolition or permanent withdrawal.

In spite of the unsatisfactory nature of the data, we may draw two tentative conclusions as to the place of the sequences of moves begun by new construction in the total housing market. First, such sequences account for the initiation of roughly half of the sequences of moves in the nation as a whole. Second, the survey estimate that about one out of four sequences begun by new construction ends in a demolition or other permanent withdrawal from stock is not obviously in error.

## B. Sequences of Moves and Statistics about Moving

There is available from the Census Bureau a widely used series based on the Current Population Survey which estimates the proportion of all individuals who move to a different house in a period of a year. In the period from March 1966 to March 1967 about 18 percent of all families moved.[4] In absolute numbers, of the approximately 58,000,000 families in the country about 10,400,000 moved. The gross number of moves, hence, is approximately known.[5]

We have just estimated the number of sequences of moves at 2,820,000 or 3,270,000. If we are prepared to assume that all moves take place as parts of sequences of moves, then the average number of moves per sequence should be of the order of 10,400,000/2,820,000 to 10,400,000/3,270,000 ie. 3.7 to 3.2. An intermediate estimate would be, say, 3.5. Sequences of moves which begin with new construction may well be somewhat longer on the average than other sequences since they tend to begin with expensive units. (See Chapter II.) The estimate from this study (Table 2) of an average of 3.5 moves for sequences beginning with new construction, however, is reasonably consistent with what is known about the total volume of moving.

We should regard this reconciliation as subject to a considerable margin of error. Refinements could be made were data at hand. Since some families move twice in one year, the number of moves per family who move in a year is undoubtedly greater than one. Also, there must be at least a few moves which are simple exchanges and do not involve sequences of the types considered in Table 15. (People may simply trade houses.) These adjustments, however, may roughly offset each other.

Another way to put the matter is to note that the estimate of 10,400,000 moves is a reasonably solid estimate based on well established procedures. The families with multiple moves will increase it only slightly. Hence, there is a ceiling on the amount of moving which can take place in the working out of sequences of moves however originated. There is also good information on the number of new housing units, and the number of deaths, so that the number of sequence beginnings is at least roughly known. There must be at least a few additions to stock from conversions and the like. The total number of sequence beginnings is unlikely to be much below 2,500,000 and is likely to be somewhat higher. Hence, an average length for sequences of moves between 3 and 4 is entirely plausible. The survey results seem consistent with existing knowledge of the housing market.

---

[4]Estimated from Current Population Reports, Population Characteristics, Series P-20, No. 171, April 30, 1968.

[5]The exact estimate is that there were in March 1967 58,493,000 families, defining as families the following: male heads of families, wife present; other male heads of primary families; male primary individuals; female heads of primary families, and female primary individuals. Of these 10,449,000 had moved to a different house in the U.S.

# 5
# Conclusions

THE purpose of this project has been to trace the indirect effects of the construction of new homes. These indirect consequences are of interest from an analytic point of view for understanding of the working of the housing market, and from a policy point of view for assessing the probable effect on the housing of the poor of measures which affect the total market for housing but do not directly affect poor families.

Do the poor benefit from new construction? It is proposed here that they benefit either if they move into new housing or if they occupy any positions in the sequences of moves begun by new construction. If they move, they benefit! This view is consistent with the conventional economic argument that people voluntarily enter into a transaction only if they expect to be better off as a result. The survey data confirm that most people who move do like their new housing better. (See Appendix Table E-22.) Even people who do not like their new quarters may benefit by being in an improved location, for example, closer to employment.

How many poor people benefit from new construction in a given period, then, depends on the volume of new construction, the length of the sequences of moves begun by by the new construction, and the proportion who are poor at each position in the sequences. There are well-known statistical series on the volume of new construction. This project was designed to yield estimates of the other two magnitudes. There has been some difficulty in estimating the average length of the sequences of moves owing to the problem of non-response in interviewing. The longer a sequence, the greater the probability that it will not be followed to its logical end. Also, some dwellings may be left vacant indefinitely before they are finally re-occupied or removed from the stock of housing. As a result of these factors the survey result is subject to some margin of uncertainty, but the most reasonable estimate of the average length of sequences of moves works out to 3.5 positions. That is, on the average for every 1000 new homes about 3500 families are able to move. This estimate cannot be checked directly against any non-survey estimate of the same magnitude. It is reasonable, however, in the light of what is known about the total number of families in the population who move in any one year and the total number of events which initiate sequences of moves, including, in addition to new construction, deaths and other factors which cause vacancies.

The proportion of families who are poor at each position in the sequences of moves is here estimated at .04 at position one, .06 at position two, and .14 at positions three, four, etc. Combining this information with the information on the length of sequences, we have an estimate that about 333 people will be poor out of the 3545 people who move as a result of the construction of 1000 new dwellings. That is, about 9.4 percent of the movers will be poor. The definition of poverty used here is that a family is poor if its income is less than $1000 plus $500 per capita for each member of the family.

Another approach to the definition of poverty is to count as poor all families below $3000 in 1965 income. In the metropolitan areas included in this study 13 percent of all families had incomes below $3000. At positions three and above in the sequences of moves about 14 percent or more of the families had incomes below $3000.

These results indicate that poor people do benefit indirectly from new construction. We can be even more optimistic when we note that roughly half of all sequences of moves are initiated by deaths, the subdivision of existing structures, emigration, and the like. Poor people presumably benefit also from these sequences. Indeed, since new dwellings are ordinarily expensive one would expect the poor to occupy a larger proportion of the positions in sequences of moves otherwise initiated.

We should not conclude from this analysis that the poor are well-provided (or ill-provided) with housing. Nor should we conclude that the price of housing is or is not reasonable. We *can* conclude that the poor are indirectly affected by the construction of new housing even if they do not occupy the new dwellings.

This conclusion, however, applies to the poor collectively. It is necessary to ask a further question: is the housing market segmented? If it is segmented, then there may be parts of the population who benefit from new construction less than in proportion to their numbers.

The housing market, one might suggest, may be segmented by age or stage in the family life cycle. It is certainly true that housing appropriate for a a very small family is not appropriate for a very large one. But the evidence in this study is that people of quite different stage in the life cycle often succeed each other in the same housing unit. In view of that fact, it is hard to see how housing could be scarce for one age group and plentiful for another.To put the same point in a different way, quarters which differ in number of rooms must be quite close substitutes.

One might also suggest that the housing market is segmented by social status. If the education of the head of a family is taken as a proxy for its status, the evidence is that housing shifts frequently from people of one status level to people of another.

Segregation by race, however, is another matter. It is well known that the income of Negroes is less than that of whites. The question at issue is whether Negroes are disadvantaged in the housing market to a greater extent than is implied by their lower incomes. The evidence is that they are indeed disadvantaged.

First, it may be asked, do Negroes move into new homes in the same proportion that one would expect on the basis of their incomes? The finding is that they do not. In fact, Negroes comprise about six-tenths of the number of occupants of new dwellings which one would predict on the basis of their incomes.

Second, Negroes in the low income group can benefit from new construction if they are able to move into a home which has been left vacant by a white family. "Trickle-down" can work if property changes from Negro to white occupancy. Such transitions do occur, but they are infrequent.

The result of these two factors is that Negroes do not benefit from new construction to the extent that their incomes would lead one to expect. We estimate that the proportion which Negroes represent of families in the sequences of moves begun by new construction is about .70 of what would be predicted on the basis of the incomes of all families in the sequences and the proportion which Negroes form of each income group in the metropolitan areas being studied.

We cannot attribute to racial discrimination the difference between .70 and 1.00. Negroes are at an economic disadvantage because of their low assets as well as their low incomes. The extent of their disadvantage in assets is indicated by the fact that their average net worth is less than a fifth of that for the population as a whole. Young Negro families are likely to be unable to obtain gifts or loans from their parents to finance the down payment on a home as well as limited in their own resources. We have not attempted to separate this factor from direct racial discimination in housing.

The findings about Negroes have various implications which may be suggested although they are not developed here systematically. They have geographical implications. New homes tend to be built on the edges of urban areas, so that the oldest part of the housing stock is near the center and the newer parts are located at increasing distances from the center. One would expect low income groups to occupy the older part of the housing supply near the center and to move outward both as their economic position improves and as the supply of housing ages. For Negroes this process seems to work imperfectly. It has implications for the supply of housing available to members of low income groups who are not subject to the same disadvantages as Negroes in the housing market. To the extent that Negroes are kept out of the market for aging housing the supply of aging houses available to others is larger than it would be otherwise.

Throughout this report we have stressed the problems of the housing of the poor. The same data can also be used to consider the importance of sequences of moves for people in the moderate income group, say, $3,000 to $6,000. The conclusion that poor people benefit indirectly from new construction applies even more strongly to those of moderate income. Those in this group made up about 19 percent of all families in the metropolitan areas studied in 1965. Although they were only 17 percent of those at position one in the sequences, they were three out of ten of those at positions two and above.

In brief, the results of the study lead to two main conclusions concerning housing policy. First, as far as low income whites are concerned, any policy which increases the total supply of housing will be beneficial. The working of the market for housing is such that the poor will benefit from any actions which increase the supply in the total market. There is a natural tendency for someone who is concerned with the provision of housing for the poor to take a direct approach. To provide housing for people, hand them the key to the door of a home! The evidence in this research is that the direct approach is not the only approach which will be effective. The housing market (for whites) operates as a single market. Any policy which shifts either the demand curve or the supply curve in the market will affect the price in the total market.

Second, Negroes are in what amounts to a partially separate market. Measures which influence the housing market as a whole, and in particular, measures which increase the supply of housing in the market as a whole, influence the market for housing for Negroes only in an attenuated form. The provision of housing for Negroes at the level which their present incomes justify will require either direct provision of more new housing units for Negro occupancy or measures which facilitate the transition of existing houses from white to Negro occupancy. It is not possible as matters now stand to rely on the sequences of moves resulting from new construction for the provision of housing for the Negro poor.

We have not attempted in this study to review the choices of policy which have been proposed or **tried as methods** of improving the supply of housing to the poor. Such a review has been undertaken recently by

Rothenberg.[1] It seems to be recognized increasingly that no single method is sufficient: a mix of programs is needed. It may be helpful, however, to state here explicitly some of the implications of this research for policies now being developed and applied.

One group of policies are intended to influence the supply of housing. One approach is to offer long term loans at below market rates of interest. While interest rates are no doubt important, for many low income people, and especially Negroes, a major obstacle to becoming home owners is the down payment requirements even when incomes may be adequate to cover monthly payments.

A second group of policies are intended to influence demand. Two methods are urged: programs to provide money which is earmarked for housing, as in rental allowances, and general subsidies to the poor, as in the negative income tax. This research shows that for Negroes these policies in themselves will not be adequate. Negroes are at a substantial disadvantage in the housing market in addition to that which results from low income.

---

[1]Jerome Rothenberg, **Economic Evaluation of Urban Renewal**, Brookings, 1967.

# Appendix A
# Sampling Building Permits

The sampling of building permits is an unusual procedure. Accordingly, in this Appendix we report our experience in some detail for the guidance of other investigators. The presentation is divided into the following sections:

1. An Overview of the Sampling Procedure;
2. The Time Lag from Issuance of Building Permit to Initial Occupancy and to the Completion of the Sequences of Moves;
3. Estimation of the Yield of Interviews from a Sample of Building Permits.

## 1. An Overview of the Sampling Procedure

The basic difficulty in developing a sample of newly-occupied homes is that there is no list of such homes. The strategy adopted in the study was to work from a sample of building permits to a sample of homes, the first occupants of the new homes representing the initial positions in the sequences of moves. Ideally, the investigators would have liked to have a sample of the dwelling units which were occupied for the first time during a specific period such as the last three months of 1965 and the first three months of 1966. The closest feasible approximation was to select a sample of building permits issued at what were estimated to be the correct intervals in advance to lead to occupancy during these periods.

The investigators were fortunate in receiving from the Census Bureau information gathered by its staff in their surveys of construction. When the study was initially planned, what was contemplated was a sample design in which in the first stage of interviewing only four metropolitan areas would be included. It proved possible to modify the plans to distribute the interviews among 17 metropolitan areas. The information obtained from the Census consisted in a list of building permit numbers, classified by metropolitan area, permit office, and date issued, and showing the number of dwellings in the building. From this list a sample was drawn. It was necessary for staff of the Survey Research Center to visit the various permit offices in order to determine the addresses corresponding to each building permit in the sample. Building permits are public documents, so that ordinarily no problems arose in obtaining permission to use them for sampling purposes.

This operation proved difficult, however, in some areas. Files of building permits, of course, are under the authority of local permit-issuing agencies, of which there may be a large number in a metropolitan area, and are organized according to practices which vary from place to place. By no means do all places file permits numerically by building permit number. It is fairly common to file permits by address, that is, by street and number. In some of the places using the latter system there is no cross-filing by building permit number. In such offices, therefore, it may be difficult or even impossible to ascertain the address to match a given permit number, so different sampling procedures were developed in these cases.

Special procedures had to be devised, also, to be used in sampling small apartment buildings and large apartment buildings, as well as structures for which the number of dwelling units was not accurately indicated on the building permit.

Initial uncertainty as to the difficulties to be encountered and the possibilities of resolving them led to a decision to undertake the field work in two stages, the first phase beginning in July 1966. Difficulties in carrying out the sampling plans in the standard metropolitan areas in the initial sample were gradually resolved. They were sufficiently troublesome, however, so that the decision was made to restrict the sample to these areas instead of adding other primary sampling units as had been contemplated.

The preference for a probability sample from a meaningful population prompted the decision to go into 17 rather than four standard metropolitan statistical areas in the first phase of the field work. Two other important considerations were the desire to utilize the Center's staff of trained interviewers located in SMSA's and the desire to utilize the sampling frame of building permits, in a sample of SMSA's, compiled by the Census Bureau. SMSA's common to the two samples included all but four of the Center's sample SMSA's with central cities of about 200,000 or more population. In order to increase representation from SMSA's outside the four largest metropolitan centers in the Northeast, the qualifying size for central cities was lowered to about 110,000 in the Northeast region.

Of the 12 largest metropolitan areas in the country four were included with certainty: the New York and Chicago consolidated areas, the Philadelphia SMSA and the Los Angeles SMSA. From the remaining eight SMSA's, a half-sample of four was chosen: Boston, Baltimore, Detroit and St. Louis.

The sample SMSA's from 18 of the Center's national sample strata (six strata from the South and four in each of the other regions) were sampled at the rate of 1 in 2 to select nine. To choose the half-sample, SMSA's were first paired according to size of central city within each region. However, some subjectivity entered into the selection of one member per pair for the first wave of the study when it was expedient to choose SMSA's where SRC supervisory staff were available, and where a sampling frame of building permits had been compiled. In four of the Center's 18 SMSA's, a prepared sampling frame did not exist; hence, in each of these cases, the matching member of the pair became the selection for the initial phase of the investigation. In two other cases, the deciding factor was the presence of supervisory staff. The nine selected SMSA's were:

In the Northeast — Syracuse, New York; and Trenton, New Jersey
In the South — Atlanta, Georgia; Miami, Florida; and Richmond, Virginia
In the West — San Diego, California; and Phoenix, Arizona.

If the second phase of the field work had been conducted in the four self-representing areas plus the half-sample of SMSA's omitted from the first phase, the selection of primary areas would have been unbiased. Because the same SMSA's were used in both phases, the sample of primary areas is biased to the extent that six of the 13 nonself-representing areas were purposively chosen. In retrospect, it seems likely that these six SMSA's would have been purposively selected even if it had been known that interviewing would be limited to only a half-sample of nonself-representing areas. Even so, it is clear that the ultimate sample of SMSA's has wider applicability than the purposive selection of four SMSA's initially proposed for the research.

Within primary sampling units it was desirable that the chains begin with a sample of primary families who were first occupants of recently constructed dwelling units. As noted above, a list of newly constructed units by date of occupancy cannot easily and inexpensively be obtained. The decision was to sample building permits issued within the following time periods:

| Type of Residential Construction | Date Building Permit Issued |
| --- | --- |
| 1. Single-family houses, and 2-4 family structures | October 1, 1964 — September 30, 1965 |
| 2. 5-29 unit apartment structures | March 1, 1964 — February 28, 1965 |
| 3. Apartment structures with 30 or more units | August 1, 1963 — July 31, 1964 |

The reason for the difference in time periods is the difference in the lag from building permit to initial occupancy for different types of construction. There were a few minor exceptions to the above time periods arising from incomplete information which led to a shorter period being sampled for some offices for some types of construction.

The departures from probability sampling methods do not appear to have been sufficiently large to introduce serious distortions in the sample. The initial sample of dwelling units, thus, is approximately a cross-section of newly-constructed homes first occupied in the last half of 1965 in metropolitan areas with medium or large population.

## 2. The Time Lag from Issuance of Building Permit to Initial Occupancy and to the Completion of Sequences of Moves

While from a sampling point of view the length of time from the date of issuance of a building permit to initial occupancy is of central importance, from a broader perspective a longer period is also important. To the analyst of the housing market it may be a matter of considerable interest to know how long it takes before the effects of new construction work themselves out. For example, he may wish to know how long it will be before a local market adjusts to the effects of the completion of a new subdivision, or a new block of apartments.

The average length of time required for an entire sequence of moves from date of building permit to occupancy of the dwelling at the last position in the sequence is shown in Table A-1 and the following tabulation:

| Type of Structure at Beginning of the Sequence | Mean Time Lag for Total Sequence |
|---|---|
| Single family house | 12.3 months |
| 2-4 family house | 14.2 months |
| Apartment | 22.4 months |

These estimates are for the completed sequences in which there was no interviewing failure. Allowing for the fact that the completed sequences tend to be shorter than the incompleted ones, we may say that the average time for the effects of a sequence begun by a new single family house to work themselves out is a little over a year — perhaps 14 months — while for sequences begun by apartments, it is about two years.

The time lags between positions in the sequences of moves are as follows:

| Type of Structure | Mean Time Lag between Positions |
|---|---|
| Single family house | 2.4 months |
| 2-4 family house | 4.8 months |
| Apartment | 4.5 months |

A sequence of moves, of course, may involve several such time lags. The distribution of time lags is skewed, so that the mean lag is substantially higher than the median (see Table A-1). Note that the lags are shorter for single family houses than for apartments.

*3. Estimation of the Yield of Interviews from a Sample of Building Permits*

The estimation of the required number of sample selections to yield the desired number of interviews at new homes for this project required answers to several questions. We had only guesses when designing the sample and calculating sampling rates for the project. These questions were:

1. What proportion of sample selections, in terms of specifically designated dwellings within structures, would be completed dwellings that could be located by interviewers?
2. What is the occupancy rate for completed dwellings?
3. What response rate may be anticipated for the occupied dwellings?

We present below answers to these questions based on our experience. The tabulations are presented in sufficient detail to show variations in the preceding rates by type of structure and size (population) of SMSA and reasons for nonresponse as well as the overall nonresponse rate.

Data for these tabulations, which relate to the new homes only, were obtained from the sample books and from records within the sampling section. Since these tabulations are based on a completely independent accounting, we have not attempted to remove the discrepancy between the total of 1133 interviews shown below and the count of 1144 interviews reported in the tabulations. The principal reason for this discrepancy is that 11 sequences "split." A "split" occurs when there are two or more vacancies as a result of people from different dwellings moving into a single dwelling. The method of tabulating the information concerning the sequences required duplication of the information for the dwelling at the position to the split. Nine of the duplicates are at position one.

Two basic tables have been prepared:
Table A-2, Percent Distributions of Sample Selections, by Classification, Type of Structure, and Size of SMSAs, in Conterminous United States, 1966.
Table A-3, Percent Distributions of Sample Dwellings, Interviews, and Noninterviews, by Type of Structure and Size of SMSAs, in Conterminous United States, 1966.

Each set contains four tables: one for the summary over all sample areas, and one for each of three size classes of SMSA's — large, medium-sized, and smaller.[1] Each table reports data by the four size-of-structure classifications used in the sample selection, as well as for the total over-all classes.

Notice that the structure size refers to the size reported on the building permit rather than to the completed size which in a few cases differs. To locate those differences would be time consuming, while the effect on the over-all picture would, we believe, be unimportant.

The tables combine data from the two interviewing periods, July and September, inasmuch as some of the July sample, because of unresolved problems, was not interviewed until September; moreover, the two phases as individual samples have no particular analytical interest.

We may recall that the sampling frame included building permits issued during a 12-month period that was varied according to the size of the structure to be constructed. In the case of single-family houses and 2 to 4-family structures, the permit year ended nine months prior to July, 1966, the first interviewing period; for 5 to 29-unit structures, the permit year ended 16 months before interviewing began; with large apartment structures, a minimum time lapse of two years was allowed.

Let us now turn to the tables in search of answers to the design questions listed above. Notice that in each section of Table A-2, the percent distributions use total sample selections as a base. This permits us to examine the disposition of the sample cases over all SMSA's and within SMSA size groups.

*What proportion of sample selections are completed dwellings?* In Table A-2 we see that the over-all rate is 81 percent, the low figure of about 77 percent in large and in medium-sized SMSA's having been very nearly balanced by the 86 percent rate in the smaller SMSA's. By type of structure, completion rates are:

| Type of Structure | Percent of Selections that are Completed Dwellings* |
|---|---|
| Single family structure | 83 |
| Apartment structures | |
| Two to four dwellings | 65 |
| Five to 29 dwellings | 85 |
| 30 dwellings or more | 69 |

*Figures are derived from data in Table A-2

---

[1]"Large SMSAs refers to those that were self-representing in the sample for the current study: New York — Northeastern New Jersey Consolidated Area, Chicago—Northwestern Indiana Consolidated area, Los Angeles SMSA and Philadelphia SMSA. "Medium-sized" SMSAs are a subsample of the remaining eight SMSAs that are generally self-representing in the SRC national household sample. "Smaller" SMSAs vary from around 250,000 to 1,000,000 population except in the Northeast where the lower bound dropped to 110,000.

We have no logical explanation for the low completion rate on two-to-four dwelling structures. Although the figure is less stable because of the small sample size, 89 dwellings out of 137 selections, it seems probable that sampling error alone would not explain the difference of 20 percentage points between the completion rate for two-to-four-unit structures and single family structures, or between two-to-four-unit structures and five-to-29 unit structures. Perhaps the time period of nine months from permit date to interviewing period was too short and should have been lengthened to 12 or 16 months. Similarly, we might reason that for large apartment structures the time period from granting of permit to interviewing should be lengthened also.

*What proportion of sample selections are incomplete dwellings?* Incomplete construction accounts for about five percent of the sample selections over all SMSA's and in the large SMSA's as well; the rate rises to nearly 10 percent in medium-sized SMSA's and drops to around three percent in the smaller areas.

By type of structure, incomplete construction rates were around 4 percent for single family and for five-to-29-unit structures (1.8/42.6 and 1.0/27.6), while in two-to-four-unit structures and in large apartment buildings about 8 percent of the selections were structures that were not yet completed (0.7/8.1 and 1.8/21.7). Again the two-to-four-unit structures and the large apartment buildings follow a similar pattern; how much time would be needed to complete construction we do not know.

*What information is available for the remaining selections?* Completed dwellings and dwellings under construction accounted for about 86 percent of sample selections; another one percent of the selections were in structures on which construction had not been started.

About 7 percent of the selections yielded no dwellings either because the address on the building permit could not be located or because the building permit itself could not be located in order to establish the address of the building site. About 2 percent of the selections led to building permits that authorized nonresidential construction; in less than 1 percent of the cases the building permit had been cancelled.

There remains a residual category that occurs because the number of dwellings authorized by building permits tends to exceed by about 3 percent the number constructed; however, in a few cases construction exceeded the original authorization.

By size of SMSA the percentages of selection that yield no dwellings follow about the same distribution as that reported for the total sample. Although we have included the estimates in the tables, by type of structure the number of sample selections becomes too small for separate analysis.

*The interviewing experience with completed dwellings:* Given that a dwelling has been completed, our next interest is in the occupancy status. In Table A-3 we see that about 94 percent of the sample dwellings were occupied:

by size of SMSA, the rates were 92, 96, and 94 percent as we progress from large to smaller SMSA's. By type of structure occupancy rates were:

| Type of Structure | Occupancy Rate (percent)* |
|---|---|
| Single family structure | 95 |
| Apartment structures | |
| 2-4 dwellings | 87 |
| 5-29 dwellings | 94 |
| 30 dwellings or more | 91 |

*Figures are derived from Table A-3

With the exception of the two-to-four-unit structures where the rate is a little low, the occupancy rates are about the same as the average rates reported quarterly by the Census Bureau for SMSA's.

All rates in Table A-3 use total completed dwellings as a base to permit a simple analysis of the disposition of sample dwellings. Over all areas, interviews were obtained in about 83 percent of the dwellings. Six percent were vacant; at about 6 percent of the dwellings an interview was refused; in about 3 percent of the cases no one was at home; and in the remaining 2 percent of sample dwellings no interview was obtained for other reasons.

By type of structure, the proportions of completed dwellings from which interviews were obtained are: 89 percent, 80 percent, 82 percent and 70 percent, as the size varies from one unit to 30 or more units (40.8/46.0; 5.2/6.5; 23.9/29.0; 12.9/18.5). By size of SMSA, the proportions of dwellings yielding responses were 85 percent in large SMSA's, 87 percent in medium-sized SMSA's, and 79 percent in the smaller SMSA's.

Another and perhaps more meaningful presentation of response and nonresponse is to calculate rates with the number of eligible respondents as the base. In this study it is equivalent to calculating rates based on the number of occupied dwellings, because an interview was desired from a responsible adult at each occupied dwelling. The following are the response and nonresponse rates:

| Classification | All Areas | Large SMSAs | Medium-Sized SMSAs | Smaller SMSAs |
|---|---|---|---|---|
| Number of eligible respondents | 1280 | 430 | 240 | 610 |
| Percent distribution | 100.0 | 100.0 | 100.0 | 100.0 |
| Interviews | 88.5 | 92.3 | 90.8 | 84.9 |
| Noninterviews | 11.5 | 7.7 | 9.2 | 15.1 |
| Refusals | 6.8 | 4.4 | 7.1 | 8.4 |
| Not-at-homes | 2.7 | 2.3 | 1.7 | 3.3 |
| Other reasons for nonresponse | 2.0 | 0.9 | 0.4 | 3.4 |

The preceding rates are in the form used most frequently to report nonresponse.

*A review of the calculation of the sampling fraction:* The calculation of the initial sampling fraction of 1/750 was based on the following considerations:

| | |
|---|---|
| Estimated newly constructed du's in SMSA's | 1,000,000 |
| Occupancy rate | 88 percent |
| Response rate (proportion of eligible respondents granting interview) | 85 percent |
| Number of units that would yield a response (new homes) | 748,000 |
| Desired number of responses | 1,000 |

The fraction was increased from 1/750 to 1/500 after interviewing was completed (or nearly so) on the first phase and the decision had been made to exclude small SMSA's from the population. The change in the fraction is equivalent to having re-defined the estimated population to be about two-thirds of its original size, assuming other factors affecting the sampling fraction are constant. From the survey data, we have the following results that may be compared with our preliminary estimates:

| | |
|---|---|
| Estimated newly constructed dwellings (500x1368 du's) | 684,000 |
| Occupancy rate (Table A-3) | 93.6 percent |
| Response rate (from preceding section) | 88.5 percent |
| Proportion of sample dwellings yielding a response | 82.8 percent |
| Number of interviews obtained (first link in chain) | 1,133 |

The underestimation of occupancy and response rates contributed to the 13 percent increase in sample size. With an estimated population of 684,000 dwellings and with the occupancy and response rates given above, a sampling fraction to yield 1,000 interviews would be 1/I where

$$I = \frac{684,000(.936)\,(.885)}{1,000} = \frac{566,598}{1,000}$$

That is, a sampling fraction of about 1/566 would have yielded a sample of about 1,000 interviews.

We regret that an independent estimate of the study population is unavailable, for purposes of a coverage check to assess what proportion of the new construction has been missed as a result of the sampling processes we used.

# Appendix B
# The Questionnaire And
# Interviewing Procedures

The procedures used in collecting data on this project were in part procedures which are standard with the field staff of the Survey Research Center. These standard procedures have been described elsewhere and will be outlined briefly below.[1] The special problems of following sequences of moves will be discussed at somewhat more length. A final section of this Appendix reproduces the questionnaire.

*1. Standard Procedures*

Several steps were taken on this study to make easier the initial contacts of interviewers with people to be interviewed. At the beginning of the study a press release describing the survey was sent to the newspaper in the local areas in which interviewing was to be done. Interviewers were provided with a printed pamphlet, *Why Do We Ask You?*, for use either at the beginning or the end of the interview. They carried "Thank You" cards to be left with respondents. These cards identify both the interviewer and the Survey Research Center. Report request cards were also provided which respondents could use to request information about the findings of the study. Interviewers regularly contact the local police and the Better Business Bureau or Chamber of Commerce in each locality before beginning a study to explain the nature and purpose of the work.

---

[1] Interviewers' Manual, Survey Research Center, Institute for Social Research, revised edition, 1966.

## 2. *Following Sequences*

In this study special procedures were required. Ordinarily, if a dwelling unit is vacant when first visited no further calls are made. In this study interviewers continued to call back at vacant housing units just as they would at an address where people were not at home.

In most studies the addresses at which interviews are to be taken are selected in the central office and sent to the interviewers. In this study addresses after the first were obtained from the people being interviewed. For this reason the next link in a chain might or might not be within reasonable distance of the interviewer who obtained its address in an interview. The instruction was for the interviewer to use some judgement as to whether to visit the next link herself, but the general guideline was to go to addresses within 50 miles and within an hour and a half of driving time (one way) but not to visit addresses which exceeded either limit. These latter addresses were sent to the Ann Arbor office along with the interviews taken at earlier links in the chain. In the office those chains which could be followed farther were divided into three categories, those to be approached by another interviewer, those to be approached by telephone, and those to be approached by mail. The priority system was in that order. That is, if the new address was within roughly 50 miles of any of the interviewers on the Center's national field staff anywhere in the United States, that interviewer was asked to visit it. If not, a telephone call was made from Ann Arbor whenever enough information was available to do so. (The people who moved out might or might not have been able to supply the name or telephone number of those who subsequently moved in.) If a telephone call could not be made, a brief questionnaire was sent by mail.

These procedures were modified in the later stages of the work. The telephone interviews proved highly successful whenever they could be made. The response rate was at least equal to that on personal interviews and the information was equally complete, except for the fact that it was not possible to observe the race of the respondent. Interviewers were permitted, therefore, to use the telephone to complete chains in the later phases of the study. A total of 228 interviews were taken by phone and 54 by mail out of the 3039 in the entire study, the remaining 2757 being personal interviews.

## 3. *The Questionnaire*

The basic questionnaire used in this investigation is the questionnaire used in personal interviews in September 1966 and thereafter. A copy appears on the following pages. This questionnaire is identical with that used in July and August 1966 except for the addition of a question sequence as to whether people moved directly from their former homes, which appears below as

Questions 9, 9a, and 9b.

In the telephone interviews the same questionnaire was used as in the personal interviews. As previously noted, however, interviewers were unable to observe the race of the respondent when interviewing by telephone.

For mail interviews a short, simplified version of the questionnaire was used. A copy appears following the basic questionnaire.

Survey Research Center                                Project 756
The University of Michigan                            September 1966

1.  ┌─────────────────────────────┐   2.  Chain Number_____
    │                             │
    │      Interviewer's Label    │   3.  Link Number_____
    │                             │
    └─────────────────────────────┘   4.  Date _____

5.  INTERVIEWER:

    List below <u>all</u> persons, including children, living in the Dwelling Unit.

                              LISTING BOX

| 5a.<br>All persons, by relation<br>or connection to head | 5b.<br>Sex | 5c.<br>Age | 5d.<br>Family<br>Unit No. | 5e.<br>Indicate Respondent<br>by Check  ✓ |
|---|---|---|---|---|
| 1.  HEAD OF DWELLING UNIT | | | 1 | |
| 2. | | | | |
| 3. | | | | |
| 4. | | | | |
| 5. | | | | |
| 6. | | | | |
| 7. | | | | |
| 8. | | | | |
| 9. | | | | |
| 10. | | | | |
| 11. | | | | |

┌─────────────────────────────────────────────────────────────────────────┐
│ INTERVIEWER:                                                              │
│   Interview any responsible adult (person aged 18 or older or married person) in │
│   Family Unit No. 1 above (Head's family).                                │
└─────────────────────────────────────────────────────────────────────────┘

6.  How many rooms do you people have in this (house, apartment), not counting bathrooms?

    _____

7.  When did you move into this (house, apartment)? _____
                                                     (MONTH)                (YEAR)
8.  We're interested in the reasons people move.  How did you happen to move here?

    _____

    _____

    _____

    _____

2.

9. Did you move here directly from your former home or did you stay someplace else for a while?

☐ MOVED DIRECTLY  ☐ STAYED SOMEPLACE ELSE

9a. Did you move in with someone, stay in a motel, rent an apartment or a house temporarily, or what?

_____

9b. How many months did you stay there? (NEAREST MONTH)

☐ LESS THAN 1    ☐ 1-2          ☐ 3-4   ☐ 5-6   ☐ OVER 6

| Not counting your temporary housing, I'd like to ask you about your last home. (GO TO Q. 9c) | I'd like to ask you about that place. (GO TO Q. 9c) |
|---|---|

9c. Was the place where you lived a private house, a 2-4 family house, an apartment in a regular apartment building, or what?

☐ PRIVATE HOUSE    ☐ 2-4 FAMILY HOUSE    ☐ OTHER (specify)_____

☐ APARTMENT IN REGULAR APARTMENT BUILDING

10. What was the address of that place?

_____
(STREET AND NUMBER)
_____
(TOWN OR CITY)                              (STATE)

11. (IF APARTMENT AND IF RESPONDENT HAS NOT ALREADY GIVEN APARTMENT NUMBER IN ADDRESS): Which apartment was it at that address? _____

12. Has somebody moved into that (house, apartment) since you moved out?

☐ YES - (GO TO Q. 13)

☐ DON'T KNOW - (SKIP TO Q. 14)

☐ NO

12a. Why not?

The D. U. was destroyed:  (CHECK THE REASON)

☐ PURPOSEFULLY DEMOLISHED (OR ABOUT TO BE)

☐ CONVERTED TO NON-RESIDENTIAL USE (OR ABOUT TO BE)    (SKIP TO Q. 17)

☐ REMODELED TO BECOME PART OF A LARGER D.U. (OR ABOUT TO BE)

☐ DESTROYED BY STORM OR FIRE

☐ OTHER (specify)_____

The D. U. was not vacated:  (CHECK THE REASON)

☐ R'S PARENTS STILL LIVE THERE

☐ R'S OTHER RELATIVES STILL LIVE THERE    (SKIP TO Q. 20)

☐ R'S ROOMMATES STILL LIVE THERE

COMMENTS (if any):_____

☐ THE D.U. IS TEMPORARILY VACANT

☐ OTHER (specify)_____    (SKIP TO Q. 14)

_____

13.  Who lives in that (house, apartment) now?              ☐ DON'T KNOW NAME

_____
                        (NAME, IF AVAILABLE)

14.  Would a person have any trouble finding the address where you used to live?

_____

_____

_____

_____

15.  After he got there, would he have any problem in knowing he had exactly the
     right place?

_____

_____

16.  We will want to get in touch with the people who moved (will move) into your
     former home, probably in person, but perhaps by phone or mail.  In case we
     should have any trouble finding them, can you tell us the name and address of
     a neighbor or someone else who could help us?
     (INTERVIEWER:  PERHAPS APARTMENT MANAGER OR REAL ESTATE AGENT)

_____

_____

17.  Compared to where you lived before, how do you like living here?

          ☐  Like it better

          ☐  About the same; better in some ways but worse in others

          ☐  Don't like it here as much

     Comments: _____

_____

_____

18.  In the (house, apartment) where you used to live, how many rooms did you people
     have, not counting bathrooms? _____

4.
19.  Did you own it or rent it or what?

☐ OWN        ☐ RENT        ☐ NEITHER  (explain)_____

_____

(IF OWNED)    19a.  About how much is it worth?              $_____

(IF RENTED)   19b.  About how much rent did you pay there?   $_____per month

20.  Now about your present home:  do you people own this home or pay rent or what?

☐ OWN        ☐ RENT        ☐ NEITHER  (explain)_____

_____

(IF OWNS)    20a.  About how much is the house worth?        $_____

(IF RENTS)   20b.  About how much rent do you pay?           $_____per month

21.  Now just a few more questions about your family:  How many years of school did
     the head of the family finish? _____

(IF MORE THAN 12)    21a.  Does he (she) have a college degree? ☐ YES    ☐ NO

22.  Approximately what was your total family income for last year - I mean 1965?
     (SHOW CARD)

A. ☐ LESS THAN $2000      D. ☐ $4000-4999        G. ☐ $7500-9999

B. ☐ $2000-2999           E. ☐ $5000-5999        H. ☐ $10,000-14,999

C. ☐ $3000-3999           F. ☐ $6000-7499        I. ☐ $15,000 OR MORE

Thank you very much for your cooperation!

_____

BY OBSERVATION:

23.  INTERVIEW WAS TAKEN AT:

/SINGLE FAMILY HOME/    /2-4 FAMILY HOME/    /APARTMENT - 5 OR MORE DWELLING/
                                             /UNITS IN BUILDING

/OTHER/   - (specify) _____

_____

24.  Race of Respondent:      ☐ WHITE      ☐ NEGRO      ☐ OTHER(specify):_____

_____

Survey Research Center                                    Project 756
University of Michigan                                     July 1966
                         Mail Questionnaire #_____

1.  Where did you live just before you moved to this address?  (Please give us the
    complete address of your former home.)

    _____

    _____

    _____

2.  Has anyone moved into the place you left?    ☐ YES    ☐ NO    ☐ DON'T KNOW

3.  What is the name of the head of the family who moved into your former home
    after you left?

    _____

    ☐ I know noone has moved in            ☐ I know someone moved in but I don't know his name

    ☐ I don't know if anyone moved in

**PLEASE CHECK THE ANSWER TO EACH OF THE FOLLOWING QUESTIONS WHICH COMES CLOSEST
TO DESCRIBING YOUR FAMILY SITUATION:**

4.  How many people are there in your family here, including children?

    ☐ 1 person
    ☐ 2 people
    ☐ 3 people
    ☐ 4 people
    ☐ 5 or more people

5.  Do you own your home or pay rent?    ☐ We own it    ☐ We pay rent

6.  What was your total family income last year?

    ☐ Less than $2000
    ☐ $2000-2999
    ☐ $3000-3999
    ☐ $4000-4999
    ☐ $5000-5999
    ☐ $6000-7499
    ☐ $7500 or more

7.  If you would like a copy of a report on the results of this study, please
    check here:
                        ☐

# Appendix C
# The Mechanics Of Transitions
# Between Housing Units:
# Temporary Quarters

The subject of moving into temporary quarters was forced upon the attention of the investigators early in the present investigation. It was found that often a new family was moving into a home weeks or months before the former occupants moved into their new home. For example, a family might move into the dwelling at position three in the sequence prior to the occupancy of the dwelling at position two by the former occupants of number three. Were people piling up on top of each other in these dwellings? The explanation turned out to be that people fairly often move out of their former dwelling well in advance of the time when they move into their new home. They go into temporary quarters. Thus, a family's former home may be ready for occupancy by someone else *before* the family actually moves into a new home.

In terms of the total demand for housing, however, the demand for temporary quarters is small. About 13 percent of moves involve use of temporary quarters. The length of stay in these quarters varies widely, as will be shown below, but two months is typical. The Census Bureau has found that only about 20 percent of all families in the country move in one year. If 13 percent of all movers use temporary quarters, that would be about 2.6 percent of all families. Two months is one-sixth of a year. Hence, not 2.6 percent of all "family-years" of housing are spent in temporary quarters, but one-sixth of 2.6 percent, or about 0.4 percent. As a percentage of the total demand for housing, the demand for temporary quarters must be small - even if the estimate of 0.4 percent is considerably in error. (An appreciable margin of error is possible since moves in sequences begun by new construction may not be typical of all moves.)

As a useful adjustment mechanism, a lubricant in the housing market, temporary quarters are more interesting. The number of families whose moves are facilitated may be a multiple of the number going into temporary quarters. That is, if one family finds temporary quarters, a move into the quarters which it vacates may be facilitated, and perhaps also other moves farther down the sequence. To think of temporary quarters as an adjustment mechanism is to imply two questions: when do people need temporary quarters, and what do they seem to require? Although this investigation was not designed primarily to answer there questions, some relevant information was obtained and will be presented.

Information about who uses temporary quarters appears in Table C-1. The date of the interview is relevant since the questionnaire was revised about September 1, 1966 to ask explicitly about temporary moves. It is the interviews after that date which are the basis for the estimate that 13 percent of moves involve use of temporary quarters.

The purpose of the move is relevant. Job-related moves are more likely to require use of temporary quarters than other moves (part B of Table C-1.) Moves undertaken because of a change in the number of members of the family (either the addition or the loss of a member), or moves to adjust the size of the dwelling unit to fit the size of the family, are less likely to involve use of temporary quarters. Such moves, of course, are local. As will be shown below, local moves are less likely to require use of temporary quarters than long distance moves. People make these moves deliberately, and usually are able to time them to avoid the need for temporary quarters.

The tenure status of the family after the move makes a difference (part C of Table C-1). People who wind up in a rented dwelling are less likely to spend time in temporary quarters than people buying a home.

People of any socio-economic status, as measured by the education of the head of the family, may use temporary quarters. There is some tendency, however, for their use to be more common among upper education people who move (part D of Table C-1).

The situation most likely to lead to use of temporary quarters is a long distance move. Of people whose move was from one region to another, 35 percent used temporary quarters, compared to 11 percent of those moving within a region. Similarly, of those moving between states 28 percent lived somewhere temporarily, in contrast to 10 percent of those moving within states (parts E and F, Table C-1).

These variables, of course, are interrelated. People with a good education are more likely to move from one part of the country to another than those with a lower level of education. They are also more likely to own their homes.

What type of temporary arrangements do people make? As shown below, 66 percent of the stays are two months or less:

| Length of Stay | Percent of Those Who Stayed in Temporary Quarters |
|----------------|:-----------------------------------:|
| Under 1 month | 29 |
| 1-2 months | 36 |
| 3-4 months | 11 |
| 5-6 months | 7 |
| Over 6 months | 17 |
| Total | 100 |
| Number of movers | 262 |

What type of temporary housing do people use? About half the time they simply move in with parents, relatives or friends (Table C-2). Otherwise there are three main possibilities: they may live in a motel or hotel, rent an apartment, or rent a house. Of the three, renting a house is least common. Information about factors which tend to influence the selection among these possibilities appears in Table C-2. Young people are more likely to move in with someone than those in the later stages of the life cycle. Higher income people (over $7500 a year) are less likely to move in with someone and more likely to rent a house or apartment than those with lower incomes. People who move from another region are particularly likely to stay in a motel or hotel. As one might expect, the length of stay is related to the type of quarters. Of those who stay two months or less, 24 percent live in a hotel or motel. On the other hand, people rarely rent a house for a period of two months or less.

# Appendix D
# List Of Tables And Graphs

## List of Tables

List of Graphs

# Appendix E
Tables

APPENDIX TABLE A-1

MEDIAN AND MEAN TIME LAGS BY TYPE OF STRUCTURE

| | | Type of Structure | | |
|---|---|---|---|---|
| Type of Lag (Months)[a] | All | Single Family House | 2-4 Family House | Apartment |
| Building permit to initial occupancy | | | | |
| Median lag | 10.5 | 6.7 | 9.7 | 18.6 |
| Mean lag | 12.1 | 7.2 | 11.3 | 18.1 |
| Standard deviation | 8.1 | 4.4 | 6.4 | 7.8 |
| Number of interviews | 1127 | 574 | 79 | 473 |
| Lag between positions[b] | | | | |
| Median lag | 1.8 | 1.3 | 2.0 | 2.3 |
| Mean lag | 3.6 | 2.4 | 4.8 | 4.5 |
| Standard deviation | 5.4 | 4.2 | 6.3 | 5.6 |
| Number of interviews | 1330 | 570 | 329 | 400 |
| Total lag for sequence of moves[c] | | | | |
| Median lag | 16.3 | 12.2 | 14.0 | 24.1 |
| Mean lag | 16.9 | 12.3 | 14.2 | 22.4 |
| Standard deviation | 9.2 | 6.8 | 8.0 | 8.6 |
| Number of interviews | 693 | 331 | 50 | 311 |

[a]Negative time lags excluded from the tabulation.

[b]Lag is from occupancy of home at one position to occupancy at the next. The dwelling unit is that vacated by the first family and occupied by the second. Based on interviews obtained after September 1, 1966, when revised question was introduced.

[c]Based on completed chains. Time shown is total lag from date of building permit to date of last move in the sequence. The columns refer to type of structure at the beginning of the sequences.

APPENDIX TABLE A-2

PERCENT DISTRIBUTIONS OF SAMPLE SELECTIONS, BY CLASSIFICATION, TYPE OF
STRUCTURE, AND SIZE OF SMSA'S IN CONTERMINOUS UNITED STATES, 1966

| | Expected Sample Dwellings by Type of Structure Authorized[1] | | | |
| | | | Apartment Structures | | |
| Classification | All Structures | Single Family Structures | 2-4 Dwellings | 5-29 Dwellings | 30 Dwellings or More |
|---|---|---|---|---|---|
| Expected sample dwellings | | All Sample Areas | | | |
| Number | 1687 | 718 | 137 | 466 | 366 |
| Sample selections by results of interviewers' visits to permit offices and building sites | | | | | |
| Completed dwellings | 81.1 | 37.3 | 5.3 | 23.5 | 15.0 |
| Construction incomplete | 5.3 | 1.8 | 0.7 | 1.0 | 1.8 |
| Construction not started | 0.9 | * | * | 0.4 | 0.5 |
| No dwelling authorized by permit | 1.8 | 0.8 | 0.1 | 0.2 | 0.7 |
| Unable to locate address on permit | 4.2 | 1.7 | 0.5 | 0.8 | 1.2 |
| Permit cancelled | 0.6 | * | * | 0.3 | 0.3 |
| Unable to locate permit | 2.7 | 1.1 | 0.2 | 0.7 | 0.8 |
| Excess of original authorizations over number of dwellings constructed | +3.3 | -0.3 | +1.3 | +0.8 | +1.4 |
| Expected sample dwellings | | Large SMSA's[2] | | | |
| Number | 603 | 209 | 69 | 175 | 150 |
| Sample selections by results of interviewers' visits to permit offices and building sites | | | | | |
| Completed dwellings | 77.3 | 28.5 | 9.3 | 22.9 | 16.6 |
| Construction incomplete | 5.8 | 1.8 | 0.8 | 1.2 | 2.0 |
| Construction not started | 0.5 | * | * | 0.2 | 0.3 |
| No dwelling authorized by permit | 3.0 | 1.0 | 0.2 | 0.3 | 1.5 |
| Unable to locate address on permit | 5.6 | 2.5 | 0.3 | 1.2 | 1.7 |
| Permit cancelled | 0.8 | * | 0.2 | 0.2 | 0.5 |
| Unable to locate permit | 4.6 | 1.3 | 0.5 | 1.0 | 1.8 |
| Excess of original authorizations over number of dwellings constructed | +2.3 | -0.5 | +0.2 | +2.2 | +0.5 |

APPENDIX TABLE A-2 - Continued

| | | | Expected Sample Dwellings by Type of Structure Authorized | | |
|---|---|---|---|---|---|
| | | | | Apartment Structures | |
| Classification | All Structures | Single Family Structures | 2-4 Dwellings | 5-29 Dwellings | 30 Dwellings or More |
| Expected sample dwellings | | Medium-Sized SMSA's[3] | | | |
| Number | 327 | 168 | 19 | 71 | 69 |
| Percent | 100.0 | 51.4 | 5.8 | 21.7 | 21.1 |
| Sample selections by results of interviewers' visits to permit offices and building sites | | | | | |
| Completed dwellings | 76.5 | 44.6 | 1.8 | 17.4 | 12.5 |
| Construction incomplete | 9.5 | 2.4 | 1.5 | 1.2 | 4.3 |
| Construction not started | 2.8 | * | 0.3 | 1.2 | 1.2 |
| No dwelling authorized by permit | 1.8 | 0.6 | 0.3 | 0.3 | 0.6 |
| Unable to locate permit | 4.3 | 1.2 | 0.9 | 0.6 | 1.5 |
| Permit cancelled | 0.3 | * | * | 0.3 | * |
| Unable to locate permit | 2.4 | 2.1 | * | 0.3 | * |
| Excess of original authorizations over number of dwellings constructed | +2.4 | +0.3 | +0.9 | +0.3 | +0.9 |
| Expected sample dwellings | | Smaller SMSA's[4] | | | |
| Number | 757 | 341 | 49 | 220 | 147 |
| Percent | 100.0 | 45.0 | 6.5 | 29.1 | 19.4 |
| Sample selections by results of interviewers' visits to permit offices and building sites | | | | | |
| Completed dwellings | 86.1 | 41.1 | 3.6 | 26.7 | 14.8 |
| Construction incomplete | 3.2 | 1.6 | 0.1 | 0.8 | 0.7 |
| Construction not started | 0.5 | 0.1 | * | 0.1 | 0.3 |
| No dwelling authorized by permit | 0.9 | 0.8 | * | * | 0.1 |
| Unable to locate address on permit | 3.0 | 1.2 | 0.4 | 0.7 | 0.8 |
| Permit cancelled | 0.5 | * | * | 0.4 | 0.1 |
| Unable to locate permit | 1.3 | 0.5 | * | 0.5 | 0.3 |
| Excess of original authorizations over number of dwellings constructed | +4.4 | -0.3 | +2.4 | -0.1 | +2.4 |

*Less than one-half of one percent.
[1]The size classifications of structures are according to the stratification

APPENDIX TABLE A-2 - Continued

used in the sample selection and in a few cases differ from the structure size reported by interviewers who visited building sites.

[2] Areas included in the sample were:  The New York-Northeastern New Jersey and the Chicago-Northwestern Indiana consolidated areas; the Philadelphia and the Los Angeles SMSA's.

[3] SMSA's included in the sample were:  Boston, Baltimore, Detroit and St. Louis.

[4] SMSA's included in the sample were:  Syracuse, New York; Dayton, Ohio; Atlanta, Georgia; Phoenix, Arizona; Trenton, New Jersey; Minneapolis-St. Paul, Minnesota; Miami, Florida; San Diego, California; Richmond, Virginia.

APPENDIX TABLE A-3

PERCENT DISTRIBUTIONS OF SAMPLE DWELLINGS, INTERVIEWS AND NONINTERVIEWS, BY TYPE OF STRUCTURE AND SIZE OF SMSA'S IN CONTERMINOUS UNITED STATES, 1966

| | Expected Sample Dwellings by Type of Structure Authorized[1] | | | |
| | | Apartment Structures | | |
| Classification | All Structures | Single Family Structures | 2-4 Dwellings | 5-29 Dwellings | 30 Dwellings or More |
|---|---|---|---|---|---|
| | All Sample Areas | | | | |
| Completed dwellings | | | | | |
| Number | 1368 | 629 | 89 | 397 | 253 |
| Percent | 100.0 | 46.0 | 6.5 | 29.0 | 18.5 |
| Vacant | 6.4 | 2.3 | 0.9 | 1.6 | 1.7 |
| Occupied | 93.6 | 43.7 | 5.6 | 27.4 | 16.8 |
| Interview obtained | 82.8 | 40.8 | 5.2 | 23.9 | 12.9 |
| No interview obtained | 10.7 | 2.9 | 0.4 | 3.5 | 3.9 |
| Interview refused | 6.4 | 2.0 | 0.2 | 1.8 | 2.3 |
| No one at home | 2.5 | 0.4 | 0.1 | 0.9 | 1.1 |
| Other reasons for noninterview | 1.9 | 0.5 | 0.1 | 0.8 | 0.4 |
| | Large SMSA's[2] | | | | |
| Completed dwellings | | | | | |
| Number | 466 | 172 | 56 | 138 | 100 |
| Percent | 100.0 | 36.9 | 12.0 | 29.6 | 21.5 |
| Vacant | 7.7 | 2.6 | 1.7 | 1.7 | 1.7 |
| Occupied | 92.3 | 34.3 | 10.3 | 27.9 | 19.7 |
| Interview obtained | 85.2 | 32.0 | 10.1 | 25.8 | 17.4 |
| No interview obtained | 7.1 | 2.4 | 0.2 | 2.1 | 2.4 |
| Interview refused | 4.1 | 1.1 | 0.2 | 1.5 | 1.3 |
| No one at home | 2.1 | 0.6 | * | 0.4 | 1.1 |
| Other reasons for noninterview | 0.9 | 0.9 | * | 0.2 | * |
| | Medium-Sized SMSA's[3] | | | | |
| Completed dwellings | | | | | |
| Number | 250 | 146 | 6 | 57 | 41 |
| Percent | 100.0 | 58.4 | 2.4 | 22.8 | 16.4 |
| Vacant | 4.0 | 1.6 | * | 1.2 | 1.2 |
| Occupied | 96.0 | 56.8 | 2.4 | 21.6 | 15.2 |
| Interview obtained | 87.2 | 54.8 | 2.4 | 18.8 | 11.2 |
| No interview obtained | 8.8 | 2.0 | * | 2.8 | 4.0 |
| Interview refused | 6.8 | 2.0 | * | 1.6 | 3.2 |
| No one at home | 1.6 | * | * | 0.8 | 0.8 |
| Other reasons for noninterview | 0.4 | * | * | 0.4 | * |

APPENDIX TABLE A-3 - Continued

| Classification | All Structures | Expected Sample Dwellings by Type of Structure Authorized | | | |
|---|---|---|---|---|---|
| | | Single Family Structures | Apartment Structures | | |
| | | | 2-4 Dwellings | 5-29 Dwellings | 30 Dwellings or More |
| | | Smaller SMSA's[4] | | | |
| Completed dwellings | | | | | |
| Number | 652 | 311 | 27 | 202 | 112 |
| Percent | 100.0 | 47.7 | 4.1 | 31.0 | 17.2 |
| Vacant | 6.4 | 2.3 | 0.6 | 1.7 | 1.8 |
| Occupied | 93.6 | 45.4 | 3.5 | 29.3 | 15.3 |
| Interview obtained | 79.4 | 41.7 | 2.8 | 24.5 | 10.4 |
| No interview obtained | 14.1 | 3.4 | 0.8 | 4.8 | 4.9 |
| Interview refused | 7.8 | 2.6 | 0.3 | 2.1 | 2.8 |
| No one at home | 3.1 | 0.5 | 0.2 | 1.2 | 1.2 |
| Other reasons for noninterview | 3.2 | 0.6 | 0.3 | 1.4 | 0.9 |

*Less than one-half of one percent.

[1]The size classifications of structures are according to the stratification used in the sample selection and in a few cases differ from the structure size reported by interviewers who visited building sites.

[2]Areas included in the sample were: The New York-Northeastern New Jersey and the Chicago-Northwestern Indiana consolidated areas; the Philadelphia and the Los Angeles SMSA's.

[3]SMSA's included in the sample were: Boston, Baltimore, Detroit and St. Louis.

[4]SMSA's included in the sample were: Syracuse, New York; Dayton, Ohio; Atlanta, Georgia; Phoenix, Arizona; Trenton, New Jersey; Minneapolis-St. Paul, Minnesota; Miami, Florida; San Diego, California; Richmond, Virginia.

APPENDIX TABLE C-1

WHETHER PEOPLE MOVED DIRECTLY FROM THEIR FORMER HOME TO THEIR NEW HOME

(Percentage distribution of movers)

| Characteristics of Movers | Stayed Someplace Else Temporarily | Moved Directly | Total | Number of Movers |
|---|---|---|---|---|
| A. Date of interview[a] | | | | |
| July-August 1966 | 6 | 94 | 100 | 628 |
| September-December 1966 | 13 | 87 | 100 | 2025 |
| | | | | |
| B. Purpose of move | | | | |
| Job-related move | 16 | 84 | 100 | 474 |
| Change in family composition | 5 | 95 | 100 | 165 |
| To adjust dwelling unit size | 4 | 96 | 100 | 200 |
| Other purposes | 12 | 88 | 100 | 1181 |
| | | | | |
| C. Change in tenure | | | | |
| Owned after the move: | | | | |
| Formerly owned | 13 | 87 | 100 | 383 |
| Formerly rented | 14 | 86 | 100 | 375 |
| Formerly neither | 24 | 76 | 100 | 80 |
| | | | | |
| Rented after the move: | | | | |
| Formerly owned | 9 | 91 | 100 | 123 |
| Formerly rented | 9 | 91 | 100 | 675 |
| Formerly neither | 18 | 82 | 100 | 354 |
| | | | | |
| D. Education (years) | | | | |
| 0-5 | 11 | 89 | 100 | 54 |
| 6-8 | 7 | 93 | 100 | 126 |
| 9-11 | 9 | 91 | 100 | 221 |
| 12 | 11 | 89 | 100 | 618 |
| 12 plus non-academic | 16 | 84 | 100 | 45 |
| 13-15 | 15 | 85 | 100 | 338 |
| 16 | 16 | 84 | 100 | 302 |
| Over 16 | 22 | 78 | 100 | 180 |
| | | | | |
| E. Regional character of moves | | | | |
| Moved from another region | 35 | 65 | 100 | 170 |
| Moved within the region | 11 | 89 | 100 | 1771 |
| | | | | |
| F. Interstate character of moves | | | | |
| Moved from another state | 28 | 72 | 100 | 284 |
| Moved within the state | 10 | 90 | 100 | 1657 |

[a]From September 1, 1966, on the question was: "Did you move here directly from your former home or did you stay someplace else for a while?"

APPENDIX TABLE C-2

WHERE PEOPLE STAYED TEMPORARILY

(Percentage distribution of those who stayed in temporary quarters)

| Characteristics of People Who Stayed in Temporary Quarters | Moved in with Someone | Motel or Hotel | Rented Apartment | House | Other | Total | Number of Movers |
|---|---|---|---|---|---|---|---|
| All | 49 | 17 | 20 | 10 | 4 | 100 | 219[a] |
| **A. Stage in Family Life Cycle[b]** | | | | | | | |
| Young, unmarried; young, married, no children | 61 | 14 | 22 | * | 3 | 100 | 63 |
| Married, with children, youngest under 5 | 51 | 18 | 18 | 9 | 4 | 100 | 74 |
| Married, with children, youngest 5-14 | 25 | 20 | 25 | 25 | 5 | 100 | 40 |
| Older, married; older, unmarried | 34 | 21 | 21 | 17 | 7 | 100 | 29 |
| **B. Family Income** | | | | | | | |
| Less than $4000 | 51 | 14 | 14 | 8 | 13 | 100 | 37 |
| $4000-7499 | 65 | 9 | 14 | 9 | 3 | 100 | 65 |
| $7500 or more | 38 | 21 | 26 | 13 | 2 | 100 | 101 |
| **C. Regional Character of Moves[c]** | | | | | | | |
| Moved from another region | 38 | 34 | 17 | 7 | 4 | 100 | 47 |
| Moved within the region | 49 | 13 | 22 | 12 | 4 | 100 | 158 |
| **D. Length of Stay** | | | | | | | |
| Two months or less | 49 | 24 | 19 | 4 | 4 | 100 | 137 |
| Three months or more | 49 | 5 | 22 | 19 | 4 | 100 | 79 |

*Less than one-half of one percent.

[a] Excludes 47 movers for whom the type of temporary quarters was not ascertained.

[b] The term "young" means under 45; "older" means 45 or older. The term "unmarried" includes those never married, and those widowed, separated (temporary or otherwise) or divorced. The term "no children" means no children under 18 living at home.

[c] There were also 7 families who came from a foreign country and went into temporary quarters, of whom 5 moved in with someone.

APPENDIX TABLE E-1

HOUSE VALUE FOR NEW DWELLINGS COMPARED TO HOUSE VALUE

FOR OTHER DWELLINGS

(Percentage distribution of families)

| House Value | From this Survey | | From a National Cross-Section[a] | |
| --- | --- | --- | --- | --- |
| | New Homes | All Positions[b] | All Nonfarm Home-Owning Families | All Home-Owners in Metropolitan Areas |
| Less than $15,000 | 10 | 19 | 51 | 43 |
| Less than $5000 | * | 1 | 9 | 5 |
| $5000-9999 | 1 | 4 | 19 | 15 |
| $10,000-14,999 | 9 | 14 | 23 | 23 |
| $15,000 or more | 90 | 81 | 49 | 57 |
| $15,000-19,999 | 24 | 28 | 21 | 23 |
| $20,000-24,999 | 20 | 19 | 11 | 14 |
| $25,000 or more | 46 | 34 | 17 | 20 |
| Total | 100 | 100 | 100 | 100 |
| Number of families | 566 | 1137 | 1507 | 1039 |

*Less than one-half of one percent.

[a]Source:  1966 Survey of Consumer Finances.

[b]All positions in sequences of moves begun by new construction.

APPENDIX TABLE E-2

HOUSE VALUE BY POSITION NUMBER

(Percentage distribution of owners)

| | | Position in the Sequence | | | | | |
|---|---|---|---|---|---|---|---|
| House Value | All | 1 | 2 | 3 | 4 | 5 | 6 or Higher |
| Less than $5000 | 1 | * | 1 | 2 | 3 | 3 | * |
| $5000-9999 | 4 | 1 | 5 | 10 | 6 | 15 | 14 |
| $10,000-14,999 | 14 | 9 | 22 | 21 | 30 | 12 | 7 |
| $15,000-19,999 | 28 | 24 | 30 | 27 | 28 | 32 | 57 |
| $20,000-24,999 | 19 | 20 | 19 | 18 | 14 | 15 | 9 |
| $25,000-34,999 | 21 | 28 | 15 | 12 | 13 | 23 | 11 |
| $35,000 or more | 13 | 18 | 8 | 10 | 6 | * | 2 |
| Total | 100 | 100 | 100 | 100 | 100 | 100 | 100 |
| Number of owners | 1137 | 566 | 283 | 146 | 64 | 34 | 44 |
| Median | $19,900 | $23,000 | $17,800 | $17,200 | $16,000 | $17,500 | $16,900 |
| Mean | $22,700 | $25,900 | $20,400 | $19,700 | $18,100 | $18,000 | $17,300 |

*Less than one-half of one percent.

APPENDIX TABLE E-3

RENT PAID BY FAMILIES LIVING IN NEW DWELLINGS
COMPARED TO RENT PAID BY OTHER FAMILIES
(Percentage distribution of families)

| | From this Survey | | From a National Cross-Section[a] | |
|---|---|---|---|---|
| Monthly Rent | New Homes | All Positions[b] | All Nonfarm Rent-Paying Families | All Rent-Paying Families in Metropolitan Areas |
| Less than $50 | 1 | 2 | 26 | 18 |
|   Less than $25 | * | * | 6 | 1 |
|   $25-49 | 1 | 2 | 20 | 17 |
| $50-99 | 18 | 39 | 55 | 61 |
|   $50-74 | 4 | 13 | 32 | 34 |
|   $75-99 | 14 | 26 | 23 | 27 |
| $100 or more | 81 | 59 | 19 | 21 |
| Total | 100 | 100 | 100 | 100 |
| Number of families | 508 | 1671 | 723 | 616 |

*Less than one-half of one percent.

[a]Source:  1966 Survey of Consumer Finances, special tabulation.

[b]All positions in sequences of moves begun by new construction.

APPENDIX TABLE E-4

RENT BY POSITION IN THE SEQUENCE

(Percentage distribution of renters)

| Monthly Rent | All Positions | Position | | | | | |
|---|---|---|---|---|---|---|---|
| | | 1 | 2 | 3 | 4 | 5 | 6 or Higher |
| Less than $100 | 41 | 19 | 41 | 55 | 60 | 56 | 55 |
| Less than $50 | 2 | 1 | 2 | 3 | 4 | 4 | 3 |
| $50-99 | 39 | 18 | 39 | 52 | 56 | 52 | 52 |
| $100 or more | 59 | 81 | 59 | 45 | 40 | 44 | 45 |
| $100-149 | 41 | 51 | 42 | 34 | 35 | 31 | 37 |
| $150-199 | 13 | 21 | 13 | 9 | 4 | 9 | 6 |
| $200-249 | 3 | 6 | 3 | 1 | 1 | 2 | 2 |
| $250 or more | 2 | 3 | 1 | 1 | * | 2 | * |
| Total | 100 | 100 | 100 | 100 | 100 | 100 | 100 |
| Number of renters | 1671 | 508 | 443 | 306 | 178 | 111 | 125 |
| Median | $110 | $130 | $110 | $90 | $90 | $85 | $90 |
| Mean | $115 | $135 | $115 | $100 | $95 | $100 | $100 |

*Less than one-half of one percent.

APPENDIX TABLE E-5

FAMILY INCOME AND RENT PAID, ALL RENT-PAYING FAMILIES IN METROPOLITAN AREAS

(Percentage distribution of families)

| Rent | All | 1965 Family Income | | | | | | | | | |
|------|-----|-----------|-----------|-----------|-----------|-----------|-----------|-----------|-----------|----------------|------------------|
| | | Less than $1000 | $1000 -1999 | $2000 -2999 | $3000 -3999 | $4000 -4999 | $5000 -5999 | $6000 -7499 | $7500 -9999 | $10,000 -14,999 | $15,000 or More |
| Less than $25 | 1 | 14 | 2 | 2 | 3 | 2 | 2 | * | * | * | * |
| $25-49 | 17 | 58 | 40 | 29 | 26 | 24 | 11 | 7 | 6 | 4 | * |
| $50-74 | 34 | 14 | 29 | 54 | 38 | 37 | 39 | 35 | 32 | 21 | 13 |
| $75-99 | 27 | 14 | 20 | 8 | 18 | 25 | 37 | 39 | 37 | 29 | 8 |
| $100-124 | 11 | * | 3 | 5 | 12 | 6 | 7 | 15 | 17 | 19 | 17 |
| $125-149 | 5 | * | * | 2 | 1 | 6 | 2 | 3 | 6 | 14 | 4 |
| $150 or more | 5 | * | 6 | * | 2 | * | 2 | 1 | 2 | 13 | 58 |
| Total | 100 | 100 | 100 | 100 | 100 | 100 | 100 | 100 | 100 | 100 | 100 |
| Number of families | 616 | 14 | 65 | 62 | 66 | 67 | 54 | 91 | 94 | 79 | 24 |
| Percent paying $100 or more | 21 | * | 9 | 7 | 15 | 12 | 11 | 19 | 25 | 46 | 79 |

*Less than one-half of one percent.

Source:  1966 Survey of Consumer Finances, special tabulation.

APPENDIX TABLE E-6

CHANGE IN EXPENDITURE FOR HOUSING, FAMILIES MOVING INTO NEW HOUSING
COMPARED TO ALL MOVERS IN THE SEQUENCES

(Percentage distribution of families)

| Ratio of Outlay after Move to Outlay before Move[a] | All Families | Families Moving into New Housing |
|---|---|---|
| Under 50 percent | 1 | 1 |
| 50-99 percent | 17 | 13 |
| 100-149 percent | 47 | 42 |
| 150-199 percent | 20 | 26 |
| 200-249 percent | 8 | 10 |
| 250-299 percent | 4 | 4 |
| 300 percent or more | 3 | 4 |
| Total | 100 | 100 |
| Number of families | 2134 | 837 |
| Median ratio | 127 | 139 |

[a]The ratio was computed using where needed the following system of equivalences between rent and house value:

| | House Value | Monthly Rent |
|---|---|---|
| 1. | $1-4999 | $1-49 |
| 2. | $5000-7499 | $50-74 |
| 3. | $7500-9999 | $75-99 |
| 4. | $10,000-14,999 | $100-124 |
| 5. | $15,000-19,999 | $125-149 |
| 6. | $20,000-24,999 | $150-199 |
| 7. | $25,000-34,999 | $200-249 |
| 8. | $35,000 or more | $250 or more |

APPENDIX TABLE E-7

CHANGE IN EXPENDITURE FOR HOUSING, ALL WHO OWNED BOTH BEFORE AND
AFTER THE MOVE, AND ALL WHO RENTED BOTH
BEFORE AND AFTER THE MOVE

(Percentage distribution of families)

| House Value or Rent after the Move Compared to House Value or Rent before the Move for the Same Families | All Who Owned Both before and after the Move | All Who Rented Both before and after the Move |
|---|---|---|
| Present house value or rent higher by two or more brackets | 37 | 18 |
| Present house value or rent higher by one bracket | 31 | 32 |
| House value or rent the same, within brackets | 24 | 34 |
| Present house value or rent lower by one bracket | 5 | 11 |
| Present house value or rent lower by two or more brackets | 3 | 5 |
| Total | 100 | 100 |
| Number of families | 489 | 971 |

APPENDIX TABLE E-8

BASIC DATA USED IN ESTIMATING PROPORTION OF SEQUENCES WHICH CONTINUE

| Position | Sequence Known to Continue | | Sequence Known to End | | Number of Sequences Whose Disposition is Known | No Information |
| | By Interview | By Information[a] | By Legal End | By Information[b] | | |
|---|---|---|---|---|---|---|
| One | 1146 | | | | | |
| Two | 786 | 48 | 250 | 11 | 1095 | 51 |
| Three | 495 | 39 | 191 | 10 | 735 | 51 |
| Four | 270 | 44 | 148 | 5 | 467 | 28 |
| Five | 156 | 25 | 74 | 2 | 257 | 13 |
| Six | 86 | 12 | 48 | 2 | 148 | 8 |
| Seven | 49 | 9 | 23 | 0 | 81 | 5 |
| Eight | 25 | 8 | 12 | 0 | 45 | 4 |
| Nine or more | 26 | 8 | 12 | 1 | 47 | 4 |
| Total | 3039 | 193 | 758 | 31 | 2875 | 164 |

[a] Includes both vacancies of less than a year and dwellings known to exist and to be occupied where no interview was taken.

[b] Includes vacancies of a year or more.

APPENDIX TABLE E-9

ESTIMATE OF PROPORTION OF SEQUENCES WHICH CONTINUE BEYOND EACH POSITION

| Position Number | Estimated Division between Sequences Which Continue and Sequences Which End | | | Number of Sequences Whose Disposition is Known |
|---|---|---|---|---|
| | Sequence Ends[a] | Sequence Continues[b] | Total | |
| One | 23.8 | 76.2 | 100.0 | 1095 |
| Two | 27.3 | 72.7 | 100.0 | 735 |
| Three | 32.8 | 67.2 | 100.0 | 467 |
| Four | 29.6 | 70.4 | 100.0 | 257 |
| Five | 33.8 | 66.2 | 100.0 | 148 |
| Six | 28.4 | 71.6 | 100.0 | 81 |
| Seven | 26.7 | 73.3 | 100.0 | 45 |
| Eight or more | 27.7 | 72.3 | 100.0 | 47 |

Weighted average mortality rate:   .274

Mean length of sequence:   3.5

[a] Includes sequences known to end, and vacancies of a year or more.

[b] Includes sequences known to continue by interview, and vacancies of less than a year and dwellings known to exist and to be occupied where no interview was taken.

APPENDIX TABLE E-10

MEAN NUMBER OF POSITIONS IN SEQUENCE, WITHIN RENT

OR VALUE OF THE NEW HOME

(distribution of sequences for which information is complete)

Value or Monthly Rent
of the New Home

| House Value, if Owner-Occupied | Monthly Rent, if Rented | Percent of Sequences | Number of Sequences | Mean Length of Sequence |
|---|---|---|---|---|
| Less than $10,000 | Less than $100 | 11 | 80 | 1.66 |
| $10,000-14,999 | $100-124 | 16 | 112 | 1.97 |
| $15,000-19,999 | $125-149 | 26 | 183 | 2.26 |
| $20,000-24,999 | $150-199 | 21 | 143 | 2.84 |
| $25,000-34,999 | $200-249 | 16 | 110 | 3.74 |
| $35,000 or more | $250 or more | 10 | 71 | 3.24 |
| Total | | 100 | 699 | 2.60 |

House Value

| | | | | |
|---|---|---|---|---|
| Less than $15,000 | | 7 | 26 | 2.19 |
| $15,000-19,999 | | 27 | 89 | 2.55 |
| $20,000-24,999 | | 22 | 72 | 3.00 |
| $25,000-34,999 | | 26 | 88 | 3.82 |
| $35,000 or more | | 18 | 61 | 3.34 |
| Total | | 100 | 336 | 3.10 |

Monthly Rent

| | | | | |
|---|---|---|---|---|
| Less than $100 | | 21 | 77 | 1.68 |
| $100-124 | | 24 | 89 | 1.89 |
| $125-149 | | 26 | 94 | 1.99 |
| $150-199 | | 20 | 71 | 2.68 |
| $200 or more | | 9 | 32 | 3.16 |
| Total | | 100 | 363 | 2.13 |

APPENDIX TABLE E-11

NUMBER OF SEQUENCES WHICH THEORETICALLY SURVIVE TO INDICATED POSITIONS
AND ESTIMATE OF THE NUMBER OF POOR FAMILIES WHO ARE INCLUDED IN THE
SEQUENCES OF MOVES RESULTING FROM AN INITIAL 1000 NEW HOMES,
DEPENDING ON INITIAL CHARACTERISTICS,
BASED ON ESTIMATED LOSS RATES*

A. Rent of New Home less than $150

| Position | Number at This Position | Estimated Loss Rates[a] | Loss | Percent Poor at This Position | Number Poor |
|---|---|---|---|---|---|
| 1 | 1000 | 42.2 | 422 | 8.1 | 81 |
| 2 | 578 | 42.5 | 246 | 11.5 | 66 |
| 3 | 332 | 40.7 | 135 | 15.0 | 50 |
| 4 | 197 | 40.3 | 79 | | 30 |
| 5 | 118 | | 48 | | 18 |
| 6 | 70 | | 28 | | 11 |
| 7 | 42 | | 17 | | 6 |
| 8 | 25 | | 10 | | 4 |
| 9 | 15 | | 6 | | 2 |
| 10 | 9 | | 4 | | 1 |
| 11 | 5 | | 2 | | 1 |
| 12 | 3 | | 1 | | b |
| 13 | 2 | | 1 | | b |
| 14 | 1 | | b | | b |
| Total | 2397 | | 999 | | 270 |

B. Rent of New Home $150 or More

| Position | Number at This Position | Estimated Loss Rates[a] | Loss | Percent Poor at This Position | Number Poor |
|---|---|---|---|---|---|
| 1 | 1000 | 21.9 | 219 | 4.3 | 43 |
| 2 | 781 | 21.6 | 169 | 0.0 | 0 |
| 3 | 612 | 31.9 | 195 | 9.9 | 61 |
| 4 | 417 | 27.5 | 115 | | 41 |
| 5 | 302 | | 83 | | 30 |
| 6 | 219 | | 60 | | 22 |
| 7 | 159 | | 44 | | 16 |
| 8 | 115 | | 32 | | 11 |
| 9 | 83 | | 23 | | 8 |
| 10 | 60 | | 17 | | 6 |
| 11 | 43 | | 12 | | 4 |
| 12 | 31 | | 9 | | 3 |
| 13 | 22 | | 6 | | 2 |
| 14 | 16 | | 4 | | 2 |
| 15 | 12 | | 3 | | 1 |
| 16 | 9 | | 2 | | 1 |
| 17 | 7 | | 2 | | 1 |
| 18 | 5 | | 1 | | b |
| 19 | 4 | | 1 | | b |
| 20 | 3 | | 1 | | b |
| 21 | 2 | | 1 | | b |
| 22 | 1 | | b | | b |
| Total | 3903 | | 999 | | 252 |

APPENDIX TABLE E-11 - Continued

C. Value of New Home
less than $25,000

| Position | Number at This Position | Estimated Loss Rates[a] | Loss | Percent Poor at This Position | Number Poor |
|---|---|---|---|---|---|
| 1 | 1000 | 17.4 | 174 | 1.7 | 17 |
| 2 | 826 | 25.1 | 207 | 6.6 | 55 |
| 3 | 619 | 32.4 | 201 | 14.7 | 91 |
| 4 | 418 | 30.0 | 125 | | 61 |
| 5 | 293 | | 88 | | 43 |
| 6 | 205 | | 62 | | 30 |
| 7 | 143 | | 43 | | 21 |
| 8 | 100 | | 30 | | 15 |
| 9 | 70 | | 21 | | 10 |
| 10 | 49 | | 15 | | 7 |
| 11 | 34 | | 10 | | 5 |
| 12 | 24 | | 7 | | 4 |
| 13 | 17 | | 5 | | 2 |
| 14 | 12 | | 4 | | 2 |
| 15 | 8 | | 2 | | 1 |
| 16 | 6 | | 2 | | 1 |
| 17 | 4 | | 1 | | 1 |
| 18 | 3 | | 1 | | b |
| 19 | 2 | | 1 | | b |
| 20 | 1 | | b | | b |
| Total | 3834 | | 999 | | 366 |

D. Value of New Home
$25,000 or More

| Position | Number at This Position | Estimated Loss Rates[a] | Loss | Percent Poor at This Position | Number Poor |
|---|---|---|---|---|---|
| 1 | 1000 | 7.3 | 73 | 0.9 | 9 |
| 2 | 927 | 17.5 | 162 | 3.9 | 36 |
| 3 | 765 | 28.8 | 220 | 10.8 | 83 |
| 4 | 545 | 30.0 | 164 | | 59 |
| 5 | 381 | | 114 | | 41 |
| 6 | 267 | | 80 | | 29 |
| 7 | 187 | | 56 | | 20 |
| 8 | 131 | | 39 | | 14 |
| 9 | 92 | | 28 | | 10 |
| 10 | 64 | | 19 | | 7 |
| 11 | 45 | | 14 | | 5 |
| 12 | 31 | | 9 | | 3 |
| 13 | 22 | | 7 | | 2 |
| 14 | 15 | | 5 | | 2 |
| 15 | 10 | | 3 | | 1 |
| 16 | 7 | | 2 | | 1 |
| 17 | 5 | | 2 | | 1 |
| 18 | 3 | | 1 | | b |
| 19 | 2 | | 1 | | b |
| 20 | 1 | | b | | b |
| Total | 4500 | | 999 | | 323 |

*Calculated on the assumption that sequences in which the last observed dwelling was vacant for less than a year will continue, and vacant for a year or more will be removed from the supply of housing.
[a]Based on observed rates for positions one, two, and three respectively, later positions based on an average for the remaining positions.
[b]Less than one.

APPENDIX TABLE E-12

DISTANCE FROM THE CENTER OF THE CITY OF DETROIT, FOR ALL POSITIONS OF SEQUENCES BEGUN IN DETROIT WHICH REMAINED WITHIN THE CITY

| Miles from Center of Detroit | Position in Sequence | | | | | | | | | All Positions of Sequences begun in Detroit which Remained in the City |
|---|---|---|---|---|---|---|---|---|---|---|
| | One (New Dwelling Unit) | Two | Three | Four | Five | Six | Seven | Eight | Nine | |
| 1.0-1.5 | 2 | | | 1 | | | | | 1 | 4 |
| 1.6-2.5 | | | | | | 1 | | | | 1 |
| 2.6-3.5 | | 3 | 1 | 2 | | | | | | 6 |
| 3.6-4.5 | | 4 | 5 | 1 | | | | | | 10 |
| 4.6-5.5 | | 2 | 4 | 4 | 3 | 2 | 1 | 1 | | 17 |
| 5.6-6.5 | | 2 | | 2 | | | 1 | 1 | | 6 |
| 6.6-7.5 | 1 | 3 | 1 | 1 | 1 | 1 | | | | 8 |
| 7.6-8.5 | | 4 | | | 2 | | | | | 6 |
| 8.6-9.5 | 2 | 1 | 3 | 2 | | | | | | 8 |
| 9.6-10.5 | | 7 | | 1 | | | | 1 | | 9 |
| 10.6-11.5 | 6 | 7 | | 2 | | 1 | 1 | | | 17 |
| 11.6-12.5 | 4 | 6 | 7 | 1 | 3 | | | | | 21 |
| 12.6-13.5 | 2 | 4 | | 1 | 1 | | | | | 8 |
| 13.6-14.5 | 4 | 4 | 2 | 1 | 1 | | | | | 12 |
| 14.6-15.5 | 1 | 2 | 1 | | | | | | | 4 |
| 15.6-16.5 | | 1 | 1 | 1 | | | | | | 3 |
| 16.6-17.5 | 7 | | | 2 | | | | | | 9 |
| 17.6-18.5 | 11 | 2 | 1 | 1 | | | | | | 15 |
| 18.6-19.5 | 9 | 4 | 3 | 1 | | | | | | 17 |
| 19.6-20.5 | 2 | | | | | | | | | 2 |
| 20.6-21.5 | 2 | | | 1 | 1 | 1 | | | | 5 |
| 21.6-22.5 | 4 | 1 | | | | | 1 | | | 6 |
| 22.6-23.5 | | 1 | | | | | | | | 1 |
| 23.6-24.5 | 7 | 1 | | 1 | | | | | | 9 |
| 24.6-25.5 | | 2 | 1 | 1 | 2 | 1 | | | | 7 |
| 25.6-26.5 | | 1 | | | | | | | | 1 |

APPENDIX TABLE E-12 - Continued

| Miles from Center of Detroit | Position in Sequence | | | | | | | | | All Positions of Sequences begun in Detroit which Remained in the City |
| --- | --- | --- | --- | --- | --- | --- | --- | --- | --- | --- |
| | One (New Dwelling Unit) | Two | Three | Four | Five | Six | Seven | Eight | Nine | |
| 26.6–27.5 | | 1 | | | | | | | | 1 |
| 27.6–28.5 | | | | | 1 | | | | | 1 |
| 28.6–29.5 | | | | | | | | | | 0 |
| 29.6–30.5 | 9 | 1 | 1 | | | | | | | 11 |
| 30.6–32.5 | | | | | | | | | | 0 |
| 32.6–33.5 | | 2 | 1 | 1 | | | | | | 4 |
| 33.6–36.5 | | | | 1 | | | | | | 0 |
| 36.6–37.5 | | 1 | | | | | | | | 2 |
| 37.6–38.5 | | | | | | | | | | 0 |
| 38.6–39.5 | | 1 | | | | | | | | 1 |
| Mean distance from center | 18.3 | 14.6 | 12.2 | 11.9 | 12.8 | | | 10.1 | | 14.6 |
| Median distance from center | 18.2 | 12.3 | 10.7 | 10.1 | 9.9 | | | 6.1 | | 12.9 |
| Number of positions | 73 | 61 | 37 | 26 | 18 | | | 17 | | 232 |

APPENDIX TABLE E-13

TYPE OF NEW HOME OCCUPIED BY FAMILY INCOME

(Percentage distribution of movers into new units)

| Type of New Home | All | Family Income | | | | | | | | |
| | | Less than $2000 | $2000 -2999 | $3000 -3999 | $4000 -4999 | $5000 -5999 | $6000 -7499 | $7500 -9999 | $10,000 -14,999 | $15,000 or More |
|---|---|---|---|---|---|---|---|---|---|---|
| Single family | 51 | 9 | 12 | 15 | 28 | 43 | 48 | 53 | 63 | 65 |
| 2-4 family | 7 | 6 | 12 | 6 | 19 | 7 | 8 | 7 | 6 | 1 |
| Apartment | 42 | 85 | 76 | 79 | 53 | 50 | 44 | 40 | 31 | 34 |
| Total | 100 | 100 | 100 | 100 | 100 | 100 | 100 | 100 | 100 | 100 |
| Number of families | 1034 | 33 | 26 | 48 | 47 | 82 | 131 | 238 | 289 | 140 |

APPENDIX TABLE E-14

TYPE OF NEW HOME OCCUPIED, BY INCOME AND FAMILY LIFE CYCLE[a]

(Percentage distributions of movers into new units)

| | | Family Income | | | | | |
|---|---|---|---|---|---|---|---|
| Type of New Home | All | Less than $4000 | $4000 -5999 | $6000 -9999 | $10,000 or More | | |
| Young, unmarried | | | | | | | |
| Single family | 6 | 8 | 10 | 6 | * | | |
| 2-4 family | 5 | 7 | 10 | 3 | * | | |
| Apartment | 89 | 85 | 80 | 91 | 100 | | |
| Total | 100 | 100 | 100 | 100 | 100 | | |
| Number of families | 98 | 27 | 20 | 32 | 19 | | |
| Young, married, no children | All | Less than $4000 | $4000 -5999 | $6000 -7499 | $7500 -9999 | $10,000 or More | |
| Single family | 27 | 11 | 28 | 20 | 22 | 36 | |
| 2-4 family | 7 | 11 | 11 | 8 | 6 | 6 | |
| Apartment | 66 | 78 | 61 | 72 | 72 | 58 | |
| Total | 100 | 100 | 100 | 100 | 100 | 100 | |
| Number of families | 173 | 18 | 18 | 25 | 46 | 66 | |
| Youngest child under 5 | All | Less than $5000 | $5000 -5999 | $6000 -7499 | $7500 -9999 | $10,000 -14,999 | $15,000 or More |
| Single family | 70 | 25 | 50 | 66 | 72 | 79 | 96 |
| 2-4 family | 7 | 5 | 17 | 10 | 9 | 2 | * |
| Apartment | 23 | 70 | 33 | 24 | 19 | 19 | 4 |
| Total | 100 | 100 | 100 | 100 | 100 | 100 | 100 |
| Number of families | 314 | 20 | 30 | 58 | 94 | 87 | 25 |

APPENDIX TABLE E-14 - Continued

| Type of New Home | All | Family Income | | | |
|---|---|---|---|---|---|
| | | Less than $6000 | $6000 -9999 | $10,000 -14,999 | $15,000 or More |
| Youngest child 5-18 | | | | | |
| Single family | 84 | 73 | 82 | 86 | 86 |
| 2-4 family | 4 | 4 | 7 | 5 | * |
| Apartment | 12 | 23 | 11 | 9 | 14 |
| Total | 100 | 100 | 100 | 100 | 100 |
| Number of families | 212 | 22 | 55 | 79 | 56 |

| Older, married, no children | All | Less than $4000 | $4000 -7499 | $7500 -9999 | $10,000 -14,999 | $15,000 or More |
|---|---|---|---|---|---|---|
| Single family | 38 | 22 | 44 | 35 | 41 | 46 |
| 2-4 family | 10 | 13 | 8 | 10 | 13 | 4 |
| Apartment | 52 | 65 | 48 | 55 | 46 | 50 |
| Total | 100 | 100 | 100 | 100 | 100 | 100 |
| Number of families | 151 | 23 | 25 | 31 | 46 | 26 |

| Older, unmarried | All | Less than $5000 | $5000 or More |
|---|---|---|---|
| Single family | 15 | 8 | 22 |
| 2-4 family | 8 | 12 | 4 |
| Apartment | 77 | 80 | 74 |
| Total | 100 | 100 | 100 |
| Number of families | 52 | 25 | 27 |

---

*Less than one-half of one percent.

[a]The term "young" means under 45; "older" means 45 or older. The term "unmarried" includes those never married, and those widowed, separated (temporarily or otherwise) or divorced. The term "no children" means no children under 18 living at home.

APPENDIX TABLE E-15

HOME OWNERSHIP STATUS, ALL FAMILIES IN METROPOLITAN AREAS, BY FAMILY INCOME[a]

(Percentage distribution of families)

| Home Ownership | All | 1965 Family Income | | | | | | | | | |
|---|---|---|---|---|---|---|---|---|---|---|---|
| | | Less than $1000 | $1000 -1999 | $2000 -2999 | $3000 -3999 | $4000 -4999 | $5000 -5999 | $6000 -7499 | $7500 -9999 | $10,000 -14,999 | $15,000 or More |
| Own | 60 | 35 | 36 | 44 | 39 | 41 | 52 | 58 | 68 | 76 | 86 |
| Do not own | 40 | 65 | 64 | 56 | 61 | 59 | 48 | 42 | 32 | 24 | 14 |
| Total | 100 | 100 | 100 | 100 | 100 | 100 | 100 | 100 | 100 | 100 | 100 |
| Number of families | 1721 | 34 | 125 | 131 | 120 | 121 | 128 | 227 | 306 | 338 | 191 |

Source: 1966 Survey of Consumer Finances.

[a]If one includes the whole country, 64 percent owned their homes in early 1966.

APPENDIX TABLE E-16

THE TRANSFER OF DWELLINGS BETWEEN FAMILIES AT DIFFERENT STAGES IN THE LIFE CYCLE[a]

(Percentage distribution of families who passed on a dwelling unit)

| Stage in the Life Cycle of the Family Who Moved in | All Stages | Stage in the Life Cycle of the Family Who Moved out | | | | | | | | |
| --- | --- | --- | --- | --- | --- | --- | --- | --- | --- | --- |
| | | Young, Unmarried | Young, Married | Married with Children | | | Older, Married | Older, Unmarried | Unmarried, with Children |
| | | | | Youngest under 5 | Youngest 5-14 | Youngest 15-17 | | | |
| Young, unmarried | 9 | 35 | 16 | 7 | 4 | 6 | 6 | 9 | 11 |
| Young, married | 17 | 22 | 33 | 18 | 10 | 6 | 14 | 14 | 12 |
| Married, with children | | | | | | | | | |
| Youngest under 5 | 35 | 11 | 21 | 43 | 42 | 36 | 26 | 23 | 40 |
| Youngest 5-14 | 13 | 5 | 5 | 12 | 21 | 29 | 17 | 10 | 11 |
| Youngest 15-17 | 2 | * | 1 | 2 | 3 | 2 | 3 | 3 | 1 |
| Older, married | 11 | 7 | 11 | 9 | 9 | 9 | 20 | 12 | 9 |
| Older, unmarried | 7 | 11 | 9 | 4 | 4 | 6 | 8 | 23 | 4 |
| Unmarried, with children | 6 | 9 | 4 | 5 | 7 | 6 | 6 | 6 | 12 |
| Total | 100 | 100 | 100 | 100 | 100 | 100 | 100 | 100 | 100 |
| Number of families | 1792 | 93 | 213 | 652 | 324 | 48 | 266 | 121 | 75 |
| Percent | 100 | 5 | 12 | 36 | 18 | 3 | 15 | 7 | 4 |

*Less than one-half of one percent.

[a]The term "young" means under 45; "older" means 45 or older. The term "unmarried" includes those never married, and those widowed, separated (temporarily or otherwise) or divorced. The term "no children" means no children under 18 living at home.

APPENDIX TABLE E-17

THE TRANSFER OF DWELLINGS BETWEEN FAMILIES WITH

HEADS OF FAMILIES AT DIFFERENT AGES

(Percentage distribution of families who
passed on a dwelling unit)

| Age of Head of Family Who Moved in | All | Age of Head of Family Who Moved Out | | | | | | |
|---|---|---|---|---|---|---|---|---|
| | | 18-24 | 25-34 | 35-44 | 45-54 | 55-64 | 65-74 | 75 and older |
| 18-24 | 21 | 41 | 24 | 14 | 14 | 17 | 19 | 13 |
| 25-34 | 34 | 28 | 41 | 35 | 29 | 29 | 28 | 10 |
| 35-44 | 20 | 11 | 15 | 28 | 23 | 26 | 18 | 13 |
| 45-54 | 12 | 7 | 11 | 13 | 18 | 15 | 9 | 17 |
| 55-64 | 7 | 7 | 5 | 6 | 10 | 7 | 11 | 14 |
| 65-74 | 4 | 5 | 3 | 3 | 5 | 3 | 10 | 13 |
| 75 and older | 2 | 1 | 1 | 1 | 1 | 3 | 5 | 20 |
| Total | 100 | 100 | 100 | 100 | 100 | 100 | 100 | 100 |
| Number of families | 1789 | 205 | 595 | 458 | 254 | 149 | 98 | 30 |
| Percent | 100 | 11 | 33 | 26 | 14 | 8 | 6 | 2 |

APPENDIX TABLE E-18

LEVEL OF EDUCATION OF HEAD OF FAMILY, SUCCESSIVE OCCUPANTS OF THE SAME DWELLING

(Percentage distribution of dwellings)

| Education of Head, Former Occupants | Education of Head, Present Occupants | | | | | | | | |
|---|---|---|---|---|---|---|---|---|---|
| | 0-5 Years | 6-8 Years | 9-11 Years | 12 Years | 12 Plus Non-College Training | College; No Degree (13-15 Years) | College; Graduated (16 Years) | Graduate Study (More than 16 Years) | All |
| 0-5 years | 1 | * | 1 | 1 | * | * | * | * | 3 |
| 6-8 years | 1 | 1 | 2 | 2 | * | 1 | * | * | 7 |
| 9-11 years | * | 2 | 3 | 4 | * | 2 | * | 1 | 12 |
| 12 years | 2 | 2 | 4 | 12 | 1 | 5 | 4 | 1 | 31 |
| 12 plus non-college training | * | * | * | 1 | * | 1 | * | * | 2 |
| College; no degree (13-15 years) | * | 1 | 2 | 6 | * | 4 | 3 | 2 | 18 |
| College; graduated (16 years) | * | 2 | 1 | 4 | 1 | 3 | 4 | 2 | 17 |
| Graduate study (more than 16 years) | * | * | 1 | 3 | * | 2 | 2 | 2 | 10 |
| All | 4 | 8 | 14 | 33 | 2 | 18 | 13 | 8 | 100 |

Number of dwellings 1628

*Less than one-half of one percent.

APPENDIX TABLE E-19

RENT FOR NEW HOMES, SHOWING WHITES AND NEGROES SEPARATELY
(Percentage distribution of families renting new homes)

| Monthly Rent | All | White | Negro |
|---|---|---|---|
| Less than $50 | 1 | 1 | 3 |
| $50-59 | * | * | 3 |
| $60-69 | 3 | 2 | 15 |
| $70-79 | 4 | 3 | 12 |
| $80-89 | 4 | 4 | 8 |
| $90-99 | 7 | 6 | 12 |
| $100-109 | 7 | 6 | 12 |
| $110-119 | 13 | 14 | 12 |
| $120-129 | 12 | 12 | 8 |
| $130-139 | 10 | 10 | * |
| $140-149 | 9 | 9 | 12 |
| $150-199 | 21 | 23 | 3 |
| $200-249 | 6 | 7 | * |
| $250-299 | 2 | 2 | * |
| $300 or more | * | 1 | * |
| Total | 100 | 100 | 100 |
| Number of families | 508 | 464 | 34 |
| Median | $130 | $130 | $95 |
| Mean | $135 | $135 | $95 |

*Less than one-half of one percent.

APPENDIX TABLE E-20

VALUE OF NEW OWNER-OCCUPIED HOMES,
SHOWING WHITES AND NEGROES SEPARATELY
(Percentage distribution of families
owning new homes)

| Value of House | All | White | Negro |
|---|---|---|---|
| Less than $10,000 | 1 | 1 | * |
| $10,000-19,999 | 33 | 32 | 47 |
| $20,000-29,999 | 36 | 36 | 37 |
| $30,000-39,999 | 18 | 18 | 16 |
| $40,000-49,999 | 7 | 8 | * |
| $50,000-59,999 | 2 | 2 | * |
| $60,000 or more | 3 | 3 | * |
| Total | 100 | 100 | 100 |
| Number of families | 566 | 535 | 19 |
| Median | $23,000 | $23,100 | $19,700 |
| Mean | $25,900 | $26,100 | $20,400 |

*Less than one-half of one percent.

## APPENDIX TABLE E-21

FAMILY INCOME OF FAMILIES OCCUPYING NEW DWELLINGS, BY RACE
(Percentage distribution of families occupying new dwellings)

| Family Income | All | White | Negro |
|---|---|---|---|
| Less than $4000 | 10 | 9 | 29 |
| Less than $2000 | 3 | 3 | 4 |
| $2000-2999 | 2 | 2 | 5 |
| $3000-3999 | 5 | 4 | 20 |
| $4000-5999 | 12 | 11 | 27 |
| $4000-4999 | 4 | 4 | 11 |
| $5000-5999 | 8 | 7 | 16 |
| $6000-9999 | 36 | 36 | 27 |
| $6000-7499 | 13 | 12 | 15 |
| $7500-9999 | 23 | 24 | 16 |
| $10,000 or more | 42 | 43 | 13 |
| $10,000-14,999 | 28 | 29 | 13 |
| $15,000 or more | 14 | 14 | * |
| Total | 100 | 100 | 100 |
| Number of families | 1034 | 958 | 55 |

*Less than one-half of one percent.

## APPENDIX TABLE E-22

### HOW PEOPLE LIKE LIVING IN THEIR PRESENT HOMES
### COMPARED TO THEIR PREVIOUS HOMES[a]

(Percentage distribution of movers)

| | Attitudes | | | | |
| Characteristic | Like This Home Better | Like This Home about the Same | Don't Like This Home as Much as Last One | Total | Number of Families |
|---|---|---|---|---|---|
| All | 75 | 16 | 9 | 100 | 2050 |
| A. Change in number of rooms | | | | | |
| Gained 4 or more rooms | 85 | 11 | 4 | 100 | 81 |
| Gained 3 rooms | 86 | 9 | 5 | 100 | 150 |
| Gained 2 rooms | 87 | 10 | 3 | 100 | 310 |
| Gained 1 room | 79 | 13 | 8 | 100 | 454 |
| No change | 74 | 16 | 10 | 100 | 541 |
| Lost 1 room | 68 | 22 | 10 | 100 | 231 |
| Lost 2 rooms | 51 | 27 | 22 | 100 | 134 |
| Lost 3 or more rooms | 44 | 28 | 28 | 100 | 93 |
| B. Change in tenure | | | | | |
| Rent to own | 89 | 8 | 3 | 100 | 509 |
| Own to own | 74 | 18 | 8 | 100 | 496 |
| Rent to rent | 73 | 17 | 10 | 100 | 855 |
| Own to rent | 40 | 28 | 32 | 100 | 152 |
| C. Reason for move | | | | | |
| Job-related | 64 | 20 | 16 | 100 | 468 |
| Change in family size or composition | 66 | 21 | 13 | 100 | 110 |
| To adjust size of home | 82 | 14 | 4 | 100 | 260 |
| Other reasons | 80 | 13 | 7 | 100 | 1014 |
| D. Whether moved across state lines | | | | | |
| Changed states | 56 | 22 | 22 | 100 | 272 |
| Moved within a state | 78 | 15 | 7 | 100 | 1764 |
| E. Poverty-affluence level | | | | | |
| Poor | 66 | 24 | 10 | 100 | 116 |
| Middle class | 79 | 13 | 8 | 100 | 818 |
| Affluent | 73 | 16 | 10 | 100 | 929 |
| F. Race | | | | | |
| White | 74 | 16 | 10 | 100 | 2363 |
| Negro | 82 | 12 | 6 | 100 | 170 |
| Other | 76 | 19 | 5 | 100 | 32 |
| G. Family number | | | | | |
| One | 75 | 17 | 8 | 100 | 922 |
| Two | 73 | 18 | 9 | 100 | 554 |
| Three | 73 | 13 | 14 | 100 | 295 |
| Four | 79 | 13 | 8 | 100 | 154 |
| Five | 77 | 10 | 13 | 100 | 101 |
| Six or higher | 83 | 12 | 5 | 100 | 60 |

[a] The question was: "Compared to where you lived before, how do you like living here?"

APPENDIX TABLE E-23

CHARACTERISTICS OF HOMES VACATED OR REMOVED FROM THE MARKET
AND FAMILIES WHO MOVED OUT OF THEM

| Type of Dwelling Unit | Homes Removed from Market | | | | Homes Still Vacant |
| | Purposely Demolished | Converted to Non-Residential Use | Remodeled to become Part of a Larger Dwelling Unit | All | |
|---|---|---|---|---|---|
| Single family house | 55 | 45 | 6 | 39 | 36 |
| 2-4 family house | 17 | 25 | 81 | 37 | 23 |
| Apartment | 24 | 20 | 10 | 19 | 37 |
| Other | 4 | 10 | 3 | 5 | 4 |
| Total | 100 | 100 | 100 | 100 | 100 |
| Number of cases | 53 | 20 | 31 | 104 | 81 |
| **Ownership Status** | | | | | |
| Owned | 34 | 30 | 6 | 26 | 20 |
| Rented | 63 | 60 | 84 | 68 | 80 |
| Neither | 3 | 10 | 10 | 6 | * |
| Total | 100 | 100 | 100 | 100 | 100 |
| Number of cases | 59 | 20 | 31 | 110 | 83 |
| **Monthly Rent** | | | | | |
| Less than $50 | 12 | | 12 | 12 | 9 |
| $50-59 | 6 | | 16 | 13 | 6 |
| $60-69 | 21 | | 20 | 19 | 14 |
| $70-79 | 28 | | 12 | 18 | 15 |
| $80-89 | 24 | | 12 | 20 | 12 |
| $90-99 | * | | 8 | 6 | 8 |
| $100-109 | 3 | | 12 | 7 | 8 |
| $110-119 | * | | 4 | 1 | 3 |
| $120-129 | 6 | | * | 3 | 9 |
| $130-139 | * | | 4 | 1 | 5 |
| $140-149 | * | | * | * | 5 |
| $150 or more | * | | * | * | 6 |
| Total | 100 | a | 100 | 100 | 100 |
| Median | $75 | | $70 | $70 | $85 |
| Number of cases | 33 | | 25 | 69 | 65 |

APPENDIX TABLE E-23 - Continued

| | | Homes Removed from Market | | | |
|---|---|---|---|---|---|
| Number of Rooms | Purposely Demolished | Converted to Non-Residential Use | Remodeled to become Part of a Larger Dwelling Unit | All | Homes Still Vacant |
| One or two | 7 | | 13 | 9 | 9 |
| Three | 12 | | 37 | 23 | 21 |
| Four | 16 | | 17 | 17 | 29 |
| Five | 20 | | 23 | 19 | 23 |
| Six | 20 | | 3 | 13 | 11 |
| Seven or more | 25 | | 7 | 19 | 7 |
| Total | 100 | a | 100 | 100 | 100 |
| Number of cases | 56 | | 30 | 105 | 82 |
| **Education of Head** | | | | | |
| 0-5 grades | 7 | | * | 5 | 4 |
| 6-8 grades | 23 | | 17 | 19 | 10 |
| 9-11 grades | 18 | | 17 | 22 | 10 |
| 12 grades | 38 | | 43 | 36 | 31 |
| Some college | 4 | | 17 | 7 | 22 |
| B.A. | 5 | | 6 | 6 | 18 |
| Advanced degree | 5 | | * | 5 | 5 |
| Total | 100 | a | 100 | 100 | 100 |
| Number of cases | 56 | | 30 | 104 | 78 |
| **Family Income** | | | | | |
| Less than $2000 | 4 | | 4 | 3 | 7 |
| $2000-2999 | 15 | | 7 | 14 | 8 |
| $3000-3999 | 13 | | * | 9 | 6 |
| $4000-4999 | 8 | | 11 | 8 | 7 |
| $5000-5999 | 19 | | 25 | 23 | 10 |
| $6000-7499 | 9 | | 14 | 10 | 25 |
| $7500-9999 | 13 | | 25 | 16 | 15 |
| $10,000-14,999 | 11 | | 14 | 12 | 17 |
| $15,000 or more | 8 | | * | 5 | 5 |
| Total | 100 | | 100 | 100 | 100 |
| Number of cases | 53 | | 28 | 96 | 83 |
| **Age of Head** | | | | | |
| 18-24 | 3 | | 26 | 13 | 14 |
| 25-34 | 19 | | 26 | 20 | 28 |
| 35-44 | 28 | | 29 | 29 | 28 |
| 45-54 | 28 | | 10 | 19 | 22 |
| 55-64 | 7 | | 3 | 6 | 2 |
| 65-74 | 8 | | 6 | 8 | 4 |
| 75 or older | 7 | | * | 5 | 2 |
| Total | 100 | a | 100 | 100 | 100 |
| Number of cases | 58 | | 31 | 108 | 83 |

*Less than one-half of one percent.

a Too few cases to percentagize.

# Index